W9-CTM-453

ARIZONA
THEN & NOW

TEXT AND CONTEMPORARY REPHOTOGRAPHY BY

ALLEN A. DUTTON

Allen A Dutton 2003

WESTCLIFFE PUBLISHERS

www.westcliffepublishers.com

CONTENTS

TEXT

PHOTOGRAPHS

INTRODUCTION

Vintage photographs fascinate me. More than simply delineating people and their environments, they seduce by their apparent directness and lack of artifice. Because of this quality, I am prone to accept these old images as an objective record. When I take the time to reflect, though, I am aware of the subjectivity embodied in vintage photographs. I realize that the human brain is not in any significant degree capable of objectivity. Still, as I view them, I almost involuntarily suspend that awareness.

Regardless of where photographers aim their cameras, they aim them at themselves, notable photographer and MIT instructor Minor White believed. The point White strove to impart was that whenever people take pictures—whether they are cognizant of it or not—they have a purpose, if it is no more than to finish the roll of film. Upon getting the prints or slides back, takers immediately become critics, asking themselves if they captured the spirit of the party, the beauty of the beloved, the vitality of the child, the villainy of the villain, the grandeur of the landscape, the delicacy of the bouquet. It's obvious they harbored no intent of making an objective statement.

What is it about so many of these 19th-century photographs that compels me to believe they are far more objective than contemporary imagery? Part of the answer lies with their seeming naiveté, which I so readily perceive as candor. But I am compelled to remind myself they simply lacked the tools we possess today to indulge our subjectivity. The very nature of a large, cumbersome camera loaded with woefully slow film is primarily responsible for the directness I admire. Spur-of-the-moment photographs that freeze fleeting impressions or gestures, so much a part of photography as we know it, remained out of reach with the unwieldy old technology. The photographer was also restricted by the nature of emulsion-coated glass plates, which limited the number of exposures available (an even smaller number if the photographer employed wet plates, which had to be developed before the collodion emulsion dried). With his flash illumination consisting of magnesium powder, the smoke from its combustion precluded even a second shot. To borrow a contemporary phrase: The early photographer simply did not have film to burn. The photographic process itself forced him to be more static and deliberate.

In photography's early days, viewers were dazzled by the camera's ability to capture infinite detail, far surpassing the capacity of any previous art form. Moreover, the medium's reasonable cost, in comparison to that of a painting, placed the photograph within the reach of ordinary people. Now, most people could have what previously only the wealthiest possessed—a portrait of themselves. Those who sat for a picture portrait considered photography an arcane craft that produced a transfixed physical likeness. That was all they had seen and therefore all they expected.

The nature of the process demanded that the photographer prohibit all motion within the field of his lens while the shutter was open. Any movement resulted in blur. Subjects were admonished not to twitch, blink, or allow their eyes to wander during the period of exposure, which might consume the better part of a minute. Eye movement during such a long exposure would produce the look of blindness. A smile was out of the question. When considering a photograph of my great-great-grandparents looking dour, I remind myself that I would appear much the same if I were not permitted to move or even blink for 30 seconds.

The same constraints limited the photographer when working outside the studio. A huge camera mounted on a tripod dictated a straight-on perspective that precluded the imaginative angles one easily achieves with a handheld camera. The properties of black-and-white glass plates and early film forced the photographer not just to eschew movement, but to become more cognizant of light and dark in delineating the subject. An aesthetic emerged, in the last half of the 19th and early 20th century, clustered around the lack of color and motion. It defined the photography of the period.

Even as I realize that the method as much as the photographer endowed the pictures with their compelling air of validity, I still savor old photographs. Their static directness defines the age and opens a window through which we sense the past. They impart a dimension that words alone will never achieve.

Twenty-five years ago I was profoundly influenced by a set of photographs. Historical images taken by William Henry Jackson were paired with contemporary shots of the same location. The contemporary photographer had located the exact spot where Jackson had set up his camera a century before, and from this vantage point he had made a new exposure. This rephotographic process endowed the new photograph with the same quality I so admired in old imagery. The juxtaposition of the two produced an alchemy that revealed the passage of time more directly than anything I had hitherto experienced. These paired photographs produced an effect in me, after 30 years as a photographer, as profound as any innovation in the history of the medium. As I gazed with rapt attention, the urge to undertake a similar project in Arizona suggested itself to me.

As soon as I started ferreting out old photographs for my project, I was struck by the phenomenal resolution and tonal range of many of the images. The old-time professional photographers, especially those who sold their work to the mining companies, used large-format cameras—and in some instances 8-inch panoramic cameras—with negatives that, when pieced together, measured 4 to 5 feet long. From these they produced contact prints of an exquisite quality that, 120 years later, we have not surpassed despite our technical advancement.

I was humbled as I compared the early photographers' quality of work to that of my images, which were enlarged from $2\frac{1}{4}$-by-$2\frac{1}{4}$-inch negatives. It was at this point that I recalled an observation made 70 years ago by painter and photographer Charles Sheeler: "It is amazing how photography has progressed without improving." I soon discovered that the jewel-like quality of those old prints derived principally, though not entirely, from the fact that they had not been enlarged. Even the finest enlargers erode, in a subtle though recognizable way, the essence of the negative. If I were to achieve the quality I so ardently admired, I would have to return to the tools the old-time photographers used. Accordingly, I invested in a second-hand, 8-by-10-inch Kodak commercial view camera, manufactured in the 1930s, and a Gortz Golden Dagor 300mm lens, bearing a formula

Allen A. Dutton, Canyon Diablo.
Photo by Judy Guerrero

although the general location accompanied each picture. Eventually, and with a great deal of humility, we became more discerning. Those old-time photographers had an uncanny knack for choosing a spot from which they could record the maximum amount of information with but a single exposure. We soon came to appreciate the stamina needed to carry a large camera, a weighty and cumbersome wooden tripod, and perhaps 10 glass plates in holders up a long hill and over broken country. Our equipment was lighter by half, and it still took real commitment to retrace their footsteps. When negotiating a rugged climb on aching legs, I would grump to myself that it was the early photographer's equipment, more than his dedication, that dictated he make the most of each shot. In the end, even this rationalization could not diminish my admiration for his discriminating eye and willingness to extend himself for just the right shot. To my pleasure, I soon discovered that even many snaps done by amateurs in the early 1900s, using only $3 Kodak box Brownies, were disarmingly direct and insightful.

One recurring frustration dogged Diane and me: the misidentification of some of the historic locations. We spent countless hours in fruitless searching, only to accidentally find later that the spot we hunted for was actually in another town. Despite such problems, by 1980, Diane and I had produced sufficient pairs that we could be selective in our choices as we assembled the book *Arizona Then and Now,* which was published by Silver Square Press the following year.

In time, readers suggested to me that, given Arizona's explosive growth over the years, a new *Arizona Then and Now* was in order. Although I readily admitted the need for an update, I hesitated to undertake it, recalling the prodigious effort I had invested the first time around. However, I finally convinced myself of the plausibility of such a project, just as Linda Doyle of Westcliffe Publishers called to inquire if I would be interested in undertaking a new *Arizona Then and Now*. At age 79, could I summon the requisite energy again? After some misgivings I thought, "What the hell. I'll give it my best shot." I went out in 2001 to once again rephotograph the historic locations.

Fortunately, I was able to persuade an old friend, photo historian Judy Guerrero, to come to my aid. Judy accompanied me on most of my jaunts around the state, and I remain deeply indebted to her sharp perception. Her meticulous note-keeping and research were

as important as her willingness to carry a backpack loaded with equipment. Her tenacity in finding the right spot waned only once, after a long day of largely unrequited effort. We were searching the ghostly remains of Swansea, a depressing spot hunkered in western Arizona's scrubby desert wilderness. Judy and I had gone without food for nearly eight hours. Suddenly she declared in unequivocal terms that she wanted to go home. I can easily forgive her this one lapse of tenaciousness, for Judy has been a stalwart, a true yeoman (or should that be yeowoman?) who has proven integral to the success of this project.

I must also thank my daughters, Beth and Wendy, and my wife, Mary Ann. Each took Judy's place on several of my trips into the hinterlands. All had sharpened their abilities to find locations while with me on several explorations in 1979–1980, back when I was working on the first edition of *Arizona Then and Now.* I am also indebted to my son, Nels, and Michael Quinn and Don Singer, two Grand Canyon National Park rangers, for their unstinting help.

My entire family, Judy, and I entertain but a single hope: that you, the reader, enjoy perusing this new and expanded edition of *Arizona Then and Now* half as much as we enjoyed producing it.

—**ALLEN A. DUTTON**

arrived at a century ago. After a year of concentrated effort in learning how to exploit the advantages of this apparatus, I was at last playing in the same ballpark with those veterans.

With equipment in place, I could concentrate on locating and copying old photographs from several historical resources around the state. I remain indebted to the many sources (identified when possible at the end of this book) who generously permitted me to enter archives with my copy camera and lights.

In 1979, I was still teaching photography at Phoenix College when Diane Taylor Bunting, one of my students, expressed enthusiasm for the rephotographing project. I quickly enlisted her help and took a year's leave. Unlike me, Diane was organized and appeared to relish keeping the meticulous records so vital to the success of such a project. We accumulated nearly a thousand copy negatives, which Diane carefully cataloged.

At first, we spent an inordinate amount of time searching for the exact spot where the early photographers set their tripods,

Grand Canyon, 1883

Standing, left to right: Eva Dutton, unknown, Mary Elida Dunham Dutton, Allen A. Dutton, Edward Everett Ayer. **Seated, left to right:** Dr. Miller, Julia Dutton, Emma A. Ayer, unknown.

This photograph holds tremendous personal significance for me. Two of the people in the group are my grandparents, Allen A. and Mary Elida Dunham Dutton. They arrived in the Arizona Territory in 1882 at the urging of Mary Elida's cousin, Edward Everett Ayer. By the time this picture was taken, Ayer, whose company supplied the burgeoning railroads with lumber, had already established himself as an influential businessman. Later, he would become known as a leading collector of Indian art, a student of Indian languages, and a philanthropist.

Ayer brought the group from Illinois to Flagstaff to assist him in building and operating what was to become the territory's largest sawmill. The mill cost Ayer $200,000, a figure in excess of $3 million by today's standards. Once the mill was producing more than 150,000 board-feet of lumber per day, he decided it was time to make the three-day journey to the Grand Canyon with his family. The 60-mile route from Flagstaff to the canyon's eastern end consisted of a set of wagon tracks with no facilities along the way, save for a rudimentary one at the canyon. The ladies in the photograph were reportedly the first Anglo women to visit the Grand Canyon.

Allen A. Dutton and family, 2001

Standing, left to right: Mary Ann Enloe Dutton, Lloyd Coldhurst, Wendy A. Dutton, Nels A. Dutton, Allen A. Dutton. **Seated, left to right:** David Bush, Dr. Elizabeth A. Dutton, Jeannie Dutton.

With our children and their families, my wife, Mary Ann, and I perched at the exact spot where Mary Elida and Allen Dutton stood at the rim of the Grand Canyon with their family in 1883. Grand Canyon archivist Michael Quinn identified the butte on the right-hand side of the picture, a landmark that revealed the exact location from which the 1883 photograph was taken. Michael also accompanied the group to take the picture once everyone had stepped into place.

The Grand Canyon seems to defy change. The only truly noticeable alteration since the time of the early photograph has occurred deep within its walls as the turbulent Colorado River erodes the inner gorge's ancient rock. The churning river, once laden with rusty-red earth, carved the canyon over millions of years; today the water is tinted a fine turquoise. Earth stripped from land in Wyoming, Colorado, and Utah now settles along the river's old channel at the upper end of Lake Powell. The water now surges from Glen Canyon Dam's great penstocks free of ruddy-colored mud, reflecting only the azure of Arizona's sky.

Grand Canyon, El Tovar Hotel, 1922

A staff of cowboys and Indians greeted guests at El Tovar Hotel, a first-class accommodation built as close as possible to the rim of the Grand Canyon. Most visitors during this era traveled via the Santa Fe Railroad to Williams, where they caught another train to the canyon station. The buses, which are parked in front of the hotel in the historic photo, met visitors at the station and shuttled them to the hotel.

The physical appearance of El Tovar remains essentially the same, although the cowboy and Indian greeters have faded to a dim memory. For the past 60 years, automobiles have been the preferred mode of travel to the Grand Canyon, forcing the Santa Fe to terminate its rail service here. Luckily, the railroad did not tear out the tracks, which enabled a company to reestablish train service to the canyon a decade ago. With millions of visitors crowding Grand Canyon National Park every year, reservations for a stay at El Tovar must be made months in advance.

Grand Canyon, El Tovar Hotel, circa 1906

Along with its prime location on the rim of the Grand Canyon, El Tovar Hotel's tastefully executed interior of Indian motifs and rough-hewn wood made it a favorite destination for notable visitors.

The hotel's multiple renovations lend its rooms a bright and airy feel, although the narrow hallways and uneven floors seem to preserve the building's historic nature. Despite the crowds that wander the rimwalks just feet from the hotel, a welcome quiet attends the veranda.

Grand Canyon, circa 1914

The woman in this photograph, possibly a guest at the El Tovar Hotel in the image's upper right, would have walked to this point on a primitive foot trail. She stands near the studio of the Kolb brothers, pioneer explorers and photographers who established their business at the very edge of the gorge.

Dr. Elizabeth Dutton stands at nearly the same spot as the woman in the black dress, and the El Tovar Hotel still anchors the background. Like countless visitors to Grand Canyon National Park, she and I have walked the canyon many times. Elizabeth holds this place in such esteem that she chose to be married at its edge.

Grand Canyon, 1892

Showman Buffalo Bill Cody (second from right) poses dramatically with a disparate group of travelers—possibly cast members of his famous Wild West Show. When this photograph was taken, Buffalo Bill and his party stood on private property. It wasn't until 1908 that the Grand Canyon became a national monument, and years later before the National Park Service purchased this property from John Hance. Miner and early Grand Canyon explorer Hance—the fellow behind Buffalo Bill seemingly unconcerned about the several-hundred-foot precipice just steps away—owned 160 acres of land on the canyon rim. He built a cabin and camp where tourists stayed in rustic tents with wooden floors. John Hance, storyteller extraordinaire, surely swapped tall tales with Buffalo Bill as they sat around the evening fire entertaining all within earshot.

Park rangers (from left): Ken Weber, Maia Browning (seated), Larry Eisenman, Kat Eisenman, Mary Bonacorda, Kevin Turner, Ron Short, Mike Anderson, Mike Quinn. Photograph by Don Singer.

The overall view remains the same, and the canyon appears as majestic as it was 109 years earlier. However, the growth of oak trees in the area where the original photographer stood rendered it impossible to photograph the scene from the same location without tree trunks and limbs blocking the view. Don had to photograph the group from a location 15 feet to the east in order to get a clear view.

What we perceive depends upon our point of view, figuratively as well as actually. All too often, we distort the past when viewing it through a contemporary lens.

BEGINNINGS

Hurtling through Arizona's seemingly endless, arid expanse, sealed in the refrigerated comfort of a modern automobile, tourists allow their present comfort to warp their concept of the past. They are prone to suppose that 19th-century settlers, whose only mode of transportation was horsepower or their own two legs, must have been a much tougher lot than people of today. How else could they have summoned the resolve to traverse such a desiccated, scrubby, greasewood-studded terrain in 115-degree heat that spawns mirages on the horizon?

Only upon closer examination are we convinced that early settlers in Arizona were humans very much like ourselves. They were adapted to an era when travel was slow, animals cussed, food basic, hygiene rudimentary, and dawn-to-dusk toil a necessity. All but the very privileged among them expected and endured a life dominated by arduous labor and widespread disease, in which fatigue was a constant companion.

All too few who whiz along the interstates stop to encounter the gentler and more inviting countryside and are therefore unaware that much of Arizona, though more arid than other states, is far from inhospitable. The interstates are constructed along beelines that shun the historic routes along the Colorado, Gila, Santa Cruz, Verde, Salt, Bill Williams, and other lesser rivers and streams. Those watercourses guided and nurtured the Indian, Spanish, Mexican, and later American adventurers. Long before the arrival of Europeans, tribes of hunter-gatherers practiced agriculture next to those streams. One prehistoric tribe, the Hohokam, farmed thousands of acres of land in the Salt River Valley using a sophisticated irrigation system.

The first Europeans to encounter the Southwest were the Spanish. At the end of the 16th century, Spain remained a feudal society, whereas the English, Dutch, and to a lesser degree the French were developing mercantilism and the beginnings of capitalism. Having

prospered as a result of the conquest of the Aztecs and Incas, Spain never faced the necessity of developing an economic base as had its northern European rivals. As the infusion of wealth from the New World into Spain diminished, so would go Spanish power. In an effort to retain its status, Spain strove to expand its empire in the hopes of finding another hoard of precious metal at least on par with that extracted from Peru and Mexico.

The anxiety of the Spanish made them particularly susceptible to tales of "cities of gold" in the northern territories of Mexico. Many, including the royalty, convinced themselves of the existence of the seven cities of Cibola, a repository of unrivaled treasure. This vision animated Spanish exploration.

When prospectors encountered Indians fashioning trinkets and jewelry from naturally occurring copper nuggets, they were quick to ascertain where the Indians had discovered the metal. One of these locations turned out to be Ajo, now a town just north of the Mexican border. The place was once strewn with native copper and exceedingly rich ore—rich enough to be profitable to mine and ship by pack burros to Port Isabel on the Gulf of California, where it was loaded on ships and taken around South America and across the Atlantic.

Gold and silver were still the ultimate goal, and gradually a web of wagon roads led north to service the many mines, including a small strike near Arizonac. In 1736, a deposit of silver, most of which lay on the surface, was discovered in this village west of Nogales. Some dispute the origin of the state's name, but the most likely source is the Pima Indian word *Arizonac*, meaning "little spring." Spanish mapmakers, however, dropped the "c" and wrote "Arizona" on their maps. Anglo cartographers copied place names from these maps, and it was not long before "Arizona" designated much of northern Mexico.

In tandem with their military effort, the Spanish brought Roman Catholicism into conquered territories. Missionary friars introduced farming and animal husbandry in conjunction with the building of missions. They were moderately successful in their bid to convert or at least mollify the Indians in several villages. Such significant buildings as the San Xavier del Bac and San José de Tumacácori missions, adorned with the familiar iconography of colonial Catholicism, lent an aura of magic intended, as one priest expressed it, "to impress and balm the savage heart beating in every Indian breast."

This technique, in the end, proved far less costly than the maintenance of a large garrison of soldiers periodically forced to pursue Indians through unfamiliar mountainous terrain. Friars, a few soldiers, and settlers with some livestock made their way up to the great bend of the Santa Cruz River, site of present-day Tucson. There they were halted in their tracks by Apache warriors, who found nothing appealing in the brand of religion the friars espoused. In fact, Apaches rarely found anyone appealing, be they Spanish, Mexican, or Indian, except other Apaches (and even that was often subject to question).

Eventually the Spanish, wedded as they were to the idea of their own superiority, succeeded in unraveling what little goodwill their more persuasive friars had engendered among the more docile Indians south of Tucson. Encouraged by their local shaman, whose influence was continually undermined by this new religion, the Indians rebelled, driving out the friars and leaving the missions to decay.

The first serious uprising occurred in 1751 when the Akimel O'odham tribe, led by Luis Oacpicagigua, killed two priests and more than 100 Spanish settlers. Responding to the slaughter in 1752, the Spanish built a new garrison (presidio) at Tubac and later one at Tucson. These fortifications held the Indians at bay, but for the next 75 years the Spanish settlements along the Santa Cruz were stymied and under constant threat. Along the far east flank of the river and to the north of Tucson lay the strongholds of the Apaches, who adamantly refused to cooperate with the Spanish, denying any access to their much-coveted land.

What force Spain could bring to bear evaporated with Mexican independence in 1821. The new Mexican government had no power to manage the various states, and many began functioning as semi-independent entities. Had it not been for the long-standing rivalries among various Indian tribes—and even among factions within tribes—which kept them from forming a cohesive force, perhaps all Mexican habitations along the Santa Cruz would have been wiped out.

A feud between the Manso and Pinal Apaches spared Tucson from destruction in the 1830s. Many communities along the Santa Cruz had for years offered the Apaches, notably the Mansos, rations if they would abide the existence of the Mexican farmers and ranchers. Because of such tribute, many of the Mansos had come to something approaching an accommodation with citizens of Tucson. Although they would not countenance any incursion into their territory beyond, some Mansos found it convenient to live near the town, as evidenced by the 1831 census, which listed 486 of them (more than the total number of Mexicans) in the Old Pueblo.

Some Mansos farmed small plots between Tucson and the Santa Cruz, others worked for Mexicans, and all freely moved between Tucson and the nearby mountains, where they hunted and harvested traditional native food plants. When the Pinals planned a general uprising designed to throw all Mexican settlers out of the Santa Cruz Valley, the Mansos refused to join them, largely because of an old feud. The uprising caused havoc, but without the Mansos, the Pinal foray proved unsuccessful. In this failure, we see why the Spanish, Mexicans, and Americans, even when badly outnumbered by Indians, managed to prevail.

After the Pinal uprising, Tucson still remained a collection of small adobe buildings surrounding the presidio; beyond them lay Indian encampments. The few Anglo adventurers who made their way to Tucson—mostly young, single males—found a thriving Mexican village. To fit into the culture they had to adapt to Mexican ways, and when they wished to start a family they married Mexican women. Spanish was the language of choice, Catholicism the religion of choice. Up until the time of the California Gold Rush, the Mexicanized Anglos were a minority.

Not much would transpire in Tucson until the "Indian problem" was solved. The dozen years separating the Mexican and Civil Wars imposed a hiatus on what little development the whole region experienced. The U.S. government, beset as it was by political haggling over secession and abolition, could spare few troops to fill the vacuum.

The few adventurers who traveled in the territory understood that they were on their own when it came to dealing with unfriendly Indians and outlaws on the range. The small force of troops stationed in Tucson's presidio was barely able to furnish an escort to accompany freight wagons carrying supplies to nearby mines.

When the Civil War erupted, the Confederacy sent 300 Texans as a small expeditionary force under the command of Colonel John Baylor into the New Mexico Territory, which at the time included Arizona, to secure the land for the South. The inept Baylor was replaced by General Henry Sibley, who detailed Captain Sherod Hunter to occupy Tucson. Hunter met no resistance from the people of the Old Pueblo and rode in unmolested on February 28, 1862.

California, which had entered the war on the side of the Union, sent a column under the command of Colonel Jim Carleton. It moved east from Los Angeles, crossed the Colorado River at Yuma, and then made its way up the Gila River. That spring, after a couple of skirmishes with the badly outnumbered Texans, Carleton, at the head of the California Column, approached Tucson. Aware of their approach, Hunter lowered the Confederate flag and led his small band out of town. The Californians rode in without having to fire a shot on May 20, 1862, and on February 24, 1863, the Arizona Territory was officially established.

Meanwhile, the newly appointed first territorial governor, John N. Goodwin, decided to acquaint himself with the vast territory he was to administer. A portly ex-congressman from the state of Maine, Goodwin was not impressed with the conditions he found in Arizona in 1863. The place suffered problems that no balding and bewhiskered politician, regardless of how well connected he might be, could hope to remedy. With the prerogative of choosing a site for the territorial capital, Goodwin was on the lookout for a spot that promised to spare him as much displeasure as possible.

In any objective assessment of the few towns in the Arizona Territory with populations of more than a couple of thousand, Tucson would appear to have been the most practical site for the capital. Its location placed it in line to be the first town of any size in Arizona to have a railroad. It was only a matter of time. After all, Tucson lay directly on the route that generated the Gadsden Purchase 10 years earlier, in which Mexico ceded what is now southern Arizona to

the United States. The long-established town possessed the best infrastructure in the territory—which is not implying a great deal.

Prescott, by comparison, seemed an unlikely candidate for the honor. It was far from what one would consider civilized, harboring nearly as many saloons as homes and no real church. The few citizens there had little or no sense of either community or comity. Law and order would be a problem. But, to be fair to Goodwin, there was little to stimulate enthusiasm in any Arizona settlement, so why not Prescott? After all, it was considerably cooler in the summer than its rivals: La Paz and Yuma on the Colorado River, Phoenix and Tucson in the middle of the desert.

Once the town, so conveniently close to the richest mineral district in all of Arizona, was designated the territory's capital, politics came to the fore. Early territorial legislators contended that Goodwin's decision to name Prescott the capital was arbitrary and ill advised. They pointed out that the majority of the population resided south of the Salt River, making the trip to the capital time-consuming and arduous. Northern Arizona, they contended, was a wasteland. In this regard, they hardly overstated their point. Until the arrival of the Atlantic and Pacific Railroad in the early 1880s, the region was a vast expanse of picturesque nothingness.

Prescott and the surrounding mining camps did not constitute a sufficient percentage of the territory's population to enable citizens to out-vote the southern half of the state. After three years of legislative debate, Tucson prevailed and stripped the capital from Prescott. The territorial legislature created a university in Tucson in 1885. The entire operation, dormitories and all, were contained in one modest building. (Today the number of students enrolled at the University of Arizona is four times greater than the entire population of the Arizona Territory at the time the university was founded.) Tucson's legislative victory, however, proved temporary. A decade later, the capital was returned to Prescott, where it remained for another 11 years. Then the political tides changed again. By 1889, Phoenix had the population, the muscle, and the political savvy to take—and keep—the capital.

This view features a store on Congress Street built by well-known Tucson pioneer and merchant Frederick A. Ronstadt. Tucsonians could find just about everything they wanted in this building, the most impressive in town. Items such as harnesses, wagons, and buggies — among life's essentials — were available here. As soon as electricity was available, Tucson installed carbon-arc street lamps like the one in the upper right portion of this photograph.

Ronstadt Park in downtown Tucson provides the perfect venue for sitting down and taking five. This brick entrance on Congress Street serves to remind people of the brick building it replaced. Popular singer Linda Ronstadt, a direct descendant of Frederick A. Ronstadt, must be pleased that the city has so honored him.

Congress Street has been one of Tucson's main thoroughfares for nearly two centuries. The trolley ran for more than a mile along the street. The poles on the left were for telephone wires, and the ones on the right were for electric power. A carbon-arc streetlamp, like the one at the top of this photo, had an eye hook on the bottom of the fixture; a maintenance worker could catch it with a long pole and pull the light down to adjust or replace the carbon rods.

The building on the near left appears to be the only remaining structure dating from 1910. Congress Street, now a one-way thoroughfare through downtown, is still one of the busiest streets in a city undergoing constant change. Much of the historic business and residential areas in or near downtown have given way to an arts center, high-rise offices, and urban parks. World War II impacted Tucson much as it did Phoenix, turning the areas near the rather sleepy communities into air bases for the training of pilots.

Tucson, circa 1911

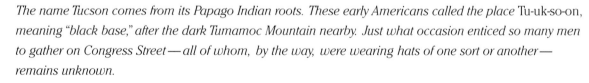

The name Tucson comes from its Papago Indian roots. These early Americans called the place Tu-uk-so-on, meaning "black base," after the dark Tumamoc Mountain nearby. Just what occasion enticed so many men to gather on Congress Street—all of whom, by the way, were wearing hats of one sort or another— remains unknown.

Congress Street, which is normally congested, appears unusually quiet for a mid-afternoon. City planners apparently decided that widening Congress Street to accommodate the constant flow of heavy daytime traffic was out of the question. By doing so, they were able to salvage a trace of the flavor of historic Tucson, one of the oldest settlements in Arizona. Nevertheless, critics contend that so much has been lost to redevelopment that whatever is left seems but a faint token of the historic street that was once the only part of Tucson considered important enough to whet the interest of pioneer photographers. The exact location of the old photograph is approximately 50 to 75 feet farther west.

Tucson, circa 1890

At the end of the 19th century, Tucson's 5,100 inhabitants made it the largest town in Arizona. The town still reflected its Spanish heritage, as seen by the large adobe structure in the center of the photo. Approximately 25 years earlier, Tucson was the most substantial Arizona community committed to the Confederacy. However, this commitment was the shortest on record — less than three months (see Beginnings, p. 11).

Tucson now devours the desert nearly as voraciously as does Phoenix. Tucson's higher elevation, however, results in cooler summers and winters, as well as modestly greater precipitation. These two factors, combined with the draw of Tucson's more verdant surrounding desert, have driven much of its growth. Unfortunately, the recent influx of newcomers threatens to eclipse Tucson's vibrant Mexican heritage, which has characterized the community since its founding by the Spanish three centuries ago.

Tumacácori, circa 1895

Italian-born cartographer, astronomer, and Jesuit missionary Father Eusebio Francisco Kino established missions in lands that are now part of northern Mexico and southern Arizona. Among them was Arizona's oldest mission, the 1691 San Cayetano de Tumacácori, relocated after the 1751 Pima Revolt and renamed San José de Tumacácori. Known for his friendly relations with the local Pima Indians, Father Kino brought cattle, sheep, and an expertise in farming to the Santa Cruz River Valley. The mission was abandoned in 1848 and left to decay because Mexico, after achieving independence from Spain, was unable to continue subsidizing it.

In 1907, a year before President Theodore Roosevelt designated Tumacácori a national monument, U.S. Forest Service inspector Coert Dubois wrote that the mission was "rapidly falling into ruins and suffering considerably from vandalism of visitors. Portions of the paintings in the old Chancel have been knocked off for souvenirs, and the whole of the inside of the nave is written over with the names of visitors." Mission preservationists opted to refurbish what remained of the adobe mission buildings, rather than rebuild them based on guesswork. Renovation efforts that began in 1919 continue today in what is now Tumacácori National Historical Park.

San Xavier del Bac, circa 1890

Father Eusebio Francisco Kino founded the San Xavier del Bac Mission in 1692, though the structure seen here dates to 1783. In the late 1760s, Charles III of Spain purged all Jesuits from Spanish lands because he distrusted the order's secular talents, so at this point the leadership of San Xavier turned over to Franciscans. Here you see the now-famous San Xavier del Bac mission at its most decrepit state. Although the Spanish crown and subsequently the fledgling Mexican government eventually withdrew the support that maintained the mission, a few Indians and Anglos have done what they could to see that San Xavier did not suffer the fate of so many missions, to keep it from falling into absolute ruin.

Seven miles south of Tucson, the adobe mission church now known as the White Dove of the Desert undergoes perpetual restoration. Adobe was made by combining straw with mud, and then packing the mixture into molds that formed bricks. Once the bricks air-dried, they were laid in tiers to fashion a wall. Because of adobe's permeability, care must be taken to ensure that water does not invade and turn the adobe back into mud. This requires that all leaks in the roof and plaster walls be eliminated. Soot from devotional candles inside the church has been cleaned from walls and statues, and whitewashing of the exterior occurs as needed. The interior's frescoes were recently restored with the help of Italian experts.

Nogales, 1890

In late 19th-century Nogales, when the border between Mexico and the United States was merely the middle of a street, anyone could cross it freely. The very thought of posting a guard or building a fence would have seemed absurd. Although Anglo miners in Bisbee, Clifton, and other mining towns protested violently when U.S. companies hired Mexican miners to break their strikes, there was little or no talk about closing the border.

What a difference 94 years can make: On both sides of the border—then marked by a chain-link fence and an immigration port—inspectors checked all who wished to cross. The inspectors spent their time collecting duties on Mexican goods (generally liquor) that Americans brought from Mexico. With no border patrol officers in evidence and so many holes in the chain-link fence, illegal crossing was simple and easy.

The change that transpired along the border during the following 22 years was even more pronounced than in the previous 94. The chain-link fence has been replaced by a 9-foot, heavy-gauge, corrugated metal barrier with 3 extra feet angled at 45 degrees toward Mexico. Border patrol activity is constant. Fragments of concrete building blocks and stones, thrown over the fence from the Mexican side, litter the American side of the border.

Tombstone, circa 1895

Fabulous silver mines spawned the town of Tombstone. Soon after, cattlemen discovered the rich rangeland that carpeted the broad valley east of the mines. The 1881 shootout at the OK Corral between lawmen Wyatt Earp and Doc Holliday, and The Clanton Gang, made Tombstone the stuff of legend.

Tourism and fantasy revived Tombstone. The town stands as gaudy testimony to the power of the Western myth. Tombstone serves up nostalgic fare along Allen Street, running parallel to State Highway 80, shown here looking south. A walk along that historic street brings visitors to the Birdcage Theater and the OK Corral, as well as other haunts of Tombstone's legendary gunslingers.

Tombstone, circa 1930

By the time this photograph of City Hall was taken, Tombstone, which now promotes itself as the "town too tough to die," had come perilously close to being cut down by the Grim Reaper's scythe. The mines had closed and Wyatt Earp, Doc Holliday, and the Clantons, who had survived the dust-up at the OK Corral in 1881, were gone. Wyatt Earp hung around until 1929 before shuffling off this mortal coil, but he did not do his hanging around in Tombstone.

The old City Hall has been refurbished and still functions as Tombstone's administrative center. Old Main Street is now State Highway 80, which runs from Bisbee to Benson. One block west, businesses cater to tourists by perpetuating the legends associated with the "town too tough to die."

Patagonia, 1900

The Spanish translation of patagon is "big paw." The mountains south of the townsite probably got their name from the large bear tracks found there by early explorers. In 1883, Rollen Richardson, lured to the area by the cattle boom, bought the Monkey Springs Ranch on Sonoita Creek. Soon he was running 12,000 head of cattle—too many for the land to sustain. A three-year drought starting in 1885 forced Richardson to sell out, but he kept 500 acres and founded a small community. Richardson wanted to name it Rollen, after himself, but the locals insisted it bear the name of the mountains to the south.

Patagonia was once prosperous enough to have a railroad, now abandoned. It connected to the San Pedro Southwestern Railroad, which joined the Southern Pacific west of Benson. By the end of World War II, Patagonia was something of a backwater. Most of the residents, descendants of the original settlers, seemed content in their unchanging community. With the great influx of people into the Salt River Valley after WWII, many of whom craved the flavor of Arizona's historic frontier, Patagonia was rediscovered. Younger professionals and retirees who have built getaway homes there now outnumber natives, and today Patagonia's pulse beats faster than ever before.

Benson, 1900

Benson, where the Southern Pacific and San Pedro Southwestern Railroads come together, sits alongside the San Pedro River and assumed importance as the shipping center of the region. According to turn-of-the-century reporter Jacob Lester, Benson's Mormon influence kept it from becoming a "hotbed of iniquity" like other nearby towns.

The Whetstone Mountains and Coronado National Forest rise on the horizon. To the north, beyond the frame of the photograph, stand the Rincon Mountains. The valley between provided an easy route for the Southern Pacific Railroad to make its way to Tucson. The railroad crossed the San Pedro River east of this shallow pass, and in the days of steam engines, water was critical for keeping the trains moving. Thus, Benson was born as a watering station next to the railway's bridge. There it prospered as a gateway for the copper-rich towns of southern Cochise County. The railroad junction is still Benson's claim to fame, though the town's importance as a shipping hub has waned since mining's boom days.

Bisbee, circa 1910

This view, looking almost directly east over the main part of downtown Bisbee, includes the lower part of Brewery Gulch. It encompasses more of this copper-mining town's residential section than any other historic picture I have come across. Hundreds of images of Bisbee still exist, for in the late 1880s through the mid-1900s, it vied for the title of the most important town in the entire territory. Note the building at the lower right of the photograph, just beyond the railroad cars. It is the railroad's roundhouse and repair facility.

The roundhouse is gone, replaced by a parking lot where tour buses unload sightseers. I took this photograph so early in the day that only one bus had arrived. Later, the lot was full. Tourism is the engine that revived the town and will likely keep it flourishing. The large "B" on the mountain dates back to when the mines still operated and the high school had enough students to make it one of the state's sports powerhouses.

Bisbee, 1907

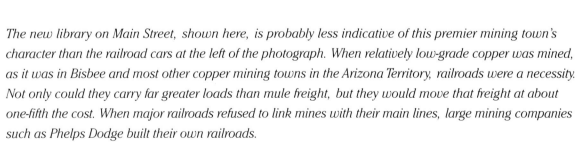

The new library on Main Street, shown here, is probably less indicative of this premier mining town's character than the railroad cars at the left of the photograph. When relatively low-grade copper was mined, as it was in Bisbee and most other copper mining towns in the Arizona Territory, railroads were a necessity. Not only could they carry far greater loads than mule freight, but they would move that freight at about one-fifth the cost. When major railroads refused to link mines with their main lines, large mining companies such as Phelps Dodge built their own railroads.

Many historic buildings in Bisbee have been preserved and maintained, although many, like the library, have changed their function. In the decades following World War II, the American public became increasingly concerned over pollution. In the face of mounting criticism of smelter emissions, and the falling ore quality in its Bisbee mines, Phelps Dodge closed both operations in 1975. When the mines shut down, the need for the railroads waned and tracks were torn up. At the time, it seemed that Bisbee might become one of Arizona's largest ghost towns. An influx of young people seeking life in a nontraditional environment discovered Bisbee. They moved in and revitalized the community.

Bisbee, circa 1907

This view of the famous Brewery Gulch represents the half of town over which Phelps Dodge could not exercise control. As the plethora of signs indicates, Brewery Gulch was a veritable beehive of activity. Unlike most of the historic images that have come down to us, the pedestrians in this photograph seemed to have had no inkling that their picture was being taken; thus we can assume this vignette was representative of normal daytime activities.

How the ubiquitous automobile has altered nearly every environment! Judging from the license plates, the majority of cars in the picture brought tourists to Bisbee. Automobiles, trees, and new civic construction made setting up a camera in the exact location where the early photographer had placed his tripod impossible. This vantage point is approximately 5 feet to the left of the original.

Bisbee, circa 1910

The complex of buildings emitting smoke, seen in the center of the photograph, sat at the heart of one of the greatest copper operations in the Arizona Territory. Take particular note of the dark line ascending the mountain at a 45-degree angle. These are the smelter's twin smokestacks—built on the side of the mountain because it was less expensive—that spewed toxic gases onto the surrounding landscape. By 1910, the fumes had stunted or killed nearly every particle of vegetation growing on the mountain. Also notice the conical mountain directly behind the smelter. Mining operations eventually consumed this feature.

Because there was no practical way for mining giant Phelps Dodge to expand the smelter at its original location, it built a state-of-the-art replacement facility nearby, and the town of Douglas was born in 1900. The company then dismantled the smelter in Bisbee and removed the stacks from the mountain. After a few years in pollution-free air, the vegetation began to recover. The mountain in the center was leveled by dynamite and giant shovels in order to extract its copper.

Douglas, 1915

Douglas rose out of the semiarid plain southeast of Bisbee when Phelps Dodge Corporation constructed a new, much larger smelter there to process the copper ore from its mines in Bisbee. The people parading down and lining Main Street (G Avenue) were Phelps Dodge employees, town businesspeople, local cowboys, and Cavalry troopers. The soldiers were stationed near the border in an effort to dissuade Pancho Villa — the same Villa that General John "Black Jack" Pershing of World War I fame failed to apprehend.

Before Phelps Dodge shut down its Douglas operation, it remodeled the company store on the northwest corner of G Avenue and 10th Street. In 1929, the Gadsden Hotel building to its right replaced the original one, which burned down. It is extremely doubtful that anything approaching the crowd seen in the historic photo could be mustered today, for Douglas' present population fails to approach that of 1915.

Douglas, 1911

As early as 1878, locals knew Douglas as Black Water. The town across the border, Agua Prieta, retains the Spanish version of that name. The muddy watering hole was used only because it was the single water source. Black Water did not become Douglas until 1901, when Dr. James Stuart Douglas, superintendent of the Phelps Dodge Mine in Sonora, convinced the company to move its smelter from Bisbee to this new location. The company dug wells and Dr. Douglas set out to build a company town. The community prospered enough to afford a streetcar line running almost the entire length of G Avenue. The first building on the right, the Gadsden Hotel, was one of the finest buildings south of the Salt River.

Although the old 1907 Gadsden Hotel burned down and was rebuilt in 1929, the lobby remains one of the most ornate a person is likely to encounter. Impressive columns support its gold-leaf ceiling, and its broad staircase is quite in keeping with the rest of the lobby. The hotel was, from the day of its completion, the most elegant building in town.

From a bank overlooking the Colorado River at Yuma, one views a sluggish squat of water; to refer to it as a "river" seems sheer hyperbole. Actually, it is but an attenuated vestige of what was once a river. In 1860, the Colorado swirled a current deep and wide enough to float paddle-wheel steamboats. It flowed untrammeled from the Grand Canyon to the Gulf of California, carrying its prodigious load of reddish-brown silt that spread a great bloom in the gulf's aquamarine water. Over eons, this mighty river deposited a massive delta which, had it not been for recurring, channel-scouring floods, might have precluded a passage deep enough for river steamers. So where did the water go?

Chronically dry Southern California had coveted Colorado River water as early as 1880. Many would-be farmers realized that the place now known as Imperial Valley had the potential to become an agricultural mecca as productive as any being developed in Arizona's Salt River Valley. All the place lacked was water. It had long been obvious that a simple gravity canal could channel Colorado River irrigation into the area, for the location lay 330 feet below sea level in a large depression west of the Colorado.

In 1897, Charles Rockwood and George Chaffey dug a 60-mile-long canal to bring water to the alkali flats coating the center of the depression known as the Salton Sink. The Colorado cooperated by remaining unusually quiescent, and by 1904 farms planted with alfalfa and cotton covered 75,000 acres. That was the year the river went on a rampage, pouring over the inadequate controls at the head of the canal and forming a nearly 100-foot waterfall. The canal continually caved as the falls retreated remorselessly back toward the Colorado, and thousands of cubic feet of water scoured its walls, turning the channel into a river itself. Had the falls reached the Colorado, all would have been lost: There would have been no way of preventing the entire flow of the mighty river from flooding down into Imperial Valley, where its water would produce a 1,000-square-mile inland sea before forging a new channel to the gulf.

The Southern Pacific Railroad, in a near panic that it would lose great sections of track, strove to dam off the flow first by dumping trainloads of boulders and finally, in a last-ditch effort, running fully loaded cars into the breach. In 1907, at a cost of $3 million (about $35 million in today's dollars), the railroad finally managed to plug the

COLORADO RIVER SETTLEMENTS

flow, but not before a 150-square-mile brackish Salton Sea had submerged many of the farms in the valley.

This near catastrophe smothered California's aspirations to tap the Colorado for almost a dozen years. Even so, the need for Colorado River water remained and a grand plan was drawn up to build a dam far upriver to not only control the floods but impound enough water to compensate for low flows. Obviously the cost would exceed the means of private investors and stymie even the State of California itself, so promoters naturally began imploring Congress to step in. Had it not been for the Great Depression of the 1930s, the project may well have remained stillborn.

The market crash of 1929 delivered the presidency to the Democratic Party, and Franklin D. Roosevelt was willing to support projects to help the nation out of its employment and economic woes. Hoover Dam promised to be a great works project that would also deliver long-sought Colorado River water to California, causing grateful Californians to rejoice. Shortly after Hoover Dam began impounding water, work started on the Imperial Dam a few miles north of Yuma. From there, an All-American Canal would deliver millions of acre-feet of the Colorado into Southern California. Over the intervening years, a succession of dams and canals have siphoned increasing amounts of water into Arizona, Nevada, and California, until the Colorado River was reduced to the pathetic vestige one encounters today at Yuma.

In 1852, when the river was a river of consequence, citizens of Yuma witnessed *Uncle Sam*, a 65-foot paddle-wheel steamboat, froth its way up the Colorado as far as the confluence of the Gila, where it ultimately ran aground and sank. Undeterred by the loss of *Uncle Sam*, the *General Jessup* replaced it two years later and so began freighting on the Colorado. By 1870, six steamboats and five barges

plied the river from the Gulf of California to the mouth of the Virgin River. Prior to 1882, only the rare piece of large mining equipment arriving in western Arizona was not transported by boat up the Colorado. A few paddle-wheelers continued to thrash their way upriver even after the Southern Pacific had bridged the Colorado at Yuma; the last was retired in 1907.

So, back to the beginnings. The Quechan Indians inhabited the Lower Colorado Valley for centuries, a domination unchallenged by either Spaniards or Mexicans. The Spanish explored the Lower Colorado as early as 1540, but it wasn't until 1775 that they established a settlement at the confluence of the Colorado and the Gila Rivers, a few miles north of present-day Yuma. As usual, the Spanish mistreated the local Quechan Indians until they rose up and killed all the adult Spanish males. The women and children fled, taking the story of the slaughter with them. The region remained exclusively Indian territory for the next 50 years.

The first forty-niners, eager to get to California, willingly paid the Quechans to swim them and their animals across the river. Although the Indians resented the Anglos as much as they had the Mexicans and the Spanish before them, the Quechans realized these interlopers weren't intent on staying, so the faster they could get them across the Colorado, the better.

Soon the trickle of travelers became a flood, large enough to make a ferry profitable. Anglos obliged. Indians objected. In 1850, Major Samuel Heintzelman established Camp Calhoun on a hill overlooking the crossing to ensure that the Quechans would not interfere with either the ferry or the travelers. Two years later, the paddle-wheeler *Uncle Sam* churned its way up from the gulf, bringing supplies to the camp. On the opposite side of the river, a civilian settlement named Colorado City grew to the point that by 1857 it warranted a post office. The name persisted until the town was renamed Yuma in 1866.

By 1855, river paddle-wheelers regularly brought troops and supplies to the fort, and transported machinery to mines along the western portion of the territory. The oceangoing vessels that brought these men and materials down from San Francisco often stopped for a day or two in Mazatlan and Guaymas for fresh victuals before arriving at Port Isabel near the mouth of the

Colorado. There, men and supplies were transferred to river steamers.

Despite the fact that those old paddle-wheelers could only make 15 miles a day against the current, they managed to transport people and supplies to Castle Dome Landing, Ehrenberg, La Paz, Parker, Hardyville, Katherine, and Rioville, a landing not far from the west end of the Grand Canyon. Ehrenberg and La Paz (now submerged by a man-made lake) were the first landings of real importance after leaving the confluence of the Colorado and the Gila. There, heavy mining machinery could be landed then reloaded into wagons and taken to numerous mines east of the river. Vulture, Stanton, Octave, Weaver, Wickenburg, Humbug, Congress, and even Phoenix depended on the riverboats and mule freighters to bring vital supplies.

By 1862, Barry Goldwater's ancestors, Joseph and Michael Goldwater, newly arrived from Europe, found scrawny and sunbaked Ehrenberg a promising enough site to build their first store and start a freighting business to supply many small communities, including Prescott. Ehrenberg, though rarely threatened by Indians, was important enough to warrant a permanent albeit small Army presence. Martha Summerhayes, a new Army bride on her way upriver, dismissed the place as "too wretched to set foot upon." She deemed even the stifling heat of the river steamer, intensified by steam boilers, preferable to going ashore. Yet when Captain Bernard, the local commanding officer stationed there, came aboard the boat to meet her, Martha refrained from any mention of the discomfort she was sure he endured. Afterwards she wrote, "I did not like to ask him how he liked his station; it seemed to me too satirical; like asking the Prisoner of Chillon, for instance, how he liked his dungeon."

Hardyville vied for the most important landing on the Colorado, as the starting point for the freight shipped to Prescott and the rich mining camps in the Bradshaw Mountains. In those years, freighting was not without risks. The road led directly through the territory of the Pias, who sporadically disrupted the freighters and occasionally murdered a few prospectors, miners, and Cavalry troopers from Fort Mohave. The Army responded with a three-year campaign during which they killed about a fourth of the tribe and destroyed nearly 70 of its camps. This slaughter, combined with outbreaks of whooping cough and dysentery, finally subdued the Pia,

forcing them to surrender by small groups in 1867 and 1868. During the campaign to eliminate their threat, the Prescott paper, in a burst of hyperbole, referred to the troopers from Fort Mohave as "The Grand Army of the Colorado."

The availability of river transportation spurred the development of mining along the banks of the Colorado. At first, most prospectors were content to pan for gold along tributaries and in the multiple washes that emptied into the Colorado. When the gold in these played out, miners moved farther and farther away from the river. By 1860, they were combing the near ranges east of the Colorado.

By 1864, rich deposits of gold, silver, lead, and zinc had been discovered on the western slope of the Cerbat Mountains. Nine mines were producing all four metals within the next 20 years. The Rainbow, Pay Roll, Georgia, Tennessee, Distaff, New Jersey, Schuylkill, Elkhart, and Hercules mines, all within an hour's walk of the small settlement of Chloride, were producing bullion. By 1900, the town had a population of 2,000, making it as big as Kingman, the county seat. Chloride was named for the prevailing form of ore, silver chloride, which the mines were tapping.

All supplies were hauled in by mule from Hardyville or Katherine Landing. Despite the presence of the Army at Fort Mohave down the river from Hardyville, the citizens of Chloride, though never attacked directly, were largely left to defend themselves during the Indian War. Eventually, enough ore was mined that the Santa Fe Railroad built a 30-mile spur to connect the town with its main line. Chloride continued to prosper until the late 1940s when, one by one, the mines closed. The abandoned Santa Fe depot remains a silent and dilapidated relic of Chloride's boom days.

Founded in 1871, Mineral Park was, like Chloride, located in the midst of one of the richest ore deposits in the Cerbat Mountains. Like its sister city, Mineral Park depended on Colorado River steamboats to link it with the outside world and on Fort Mohave, the only military post in the area, for its protection. In 1870, one traveler described the fort as being as "squalid and as Spartan an endeavour as has man or beast been fated to endure." Its few buildings were bare, sun-bleached adobe with a bit of improvised shade extending a few feet along their north sides. During the six months of summer, most of the activity, as well as all sleeping, took place under these shades.

Mineral Park was the epitome of a boom town. It mushroomed miraculously in a matter of months. Two years after its founding, the population was estimated at nearly 2,000 and the town had become the county seat in true Western style: by commandeering the county records from the Cerbat, another mining camp a few miles to the south. Citizens of Cerbat were loath to dignify the operation with such a glowing term as "commandeer." Rather they characterized it as a "purloining . . . the work of cowardly sneak thieves operating in the dead of night." Mineral Park not only held the county records, it hosted hotels, restaurants, a newspaper, the *Mohave County Miner*, bawdy houses, assay offices, and two stage coach stations. Even though the mines produced significant quantities of gold and silver, they remained at the mercy of long-distance mule freighters and the high fees charged by the river steamboat owners.

In 1883, when the Atlantic and Pacific Railroad passed through Kingman only 20 miles away, Mineral Parkers rejoiced. Although the mines would be forced to pay monopoly rates charged by the railroad, the rates would be far cheaper than the cost of river freight and the long haul by mule teams from the Colorado. Apparently they did not foresee the impact the railroad would have on the scrawny community of Kingman, which ultimately provided the only railhead for the several dozen important mines scattered around Mohave County. Unlike Winslow, with its large railroad installations, Kingman was not a railroad town. The Atlantic and Pacific, soon to be the Santa Fe, had built only a modest depot, small warehouse, and a minimal Harvey House there. Neither was Kingman a mining town. The nearest significant mine was 18 miles away. Instead it functioned as a freighting and commercial center, and in a matter of a few years Kingman had grown larger then Mineral Park—*and* it was on the railroad.

In 1887, the voters of Mohave County chose Kingman as the county seat, but citizens of Mineral Park were no more willing to surrender the county records than those in Cerbat had been. Occasionally history repeats itself. According to Mineral Parkers, the records had found their way to Kingman by "stealth and connivance." The *Mohave County Miner* soon followed and took up weekly publishing in Kingman.

Mineral Park did not possess the staying power of Chloride. The rich ore petered out and the last mine ceased production in

1901. A brief revival of two of the mines in 1906 lent a few of the town's stubborn hangers-on a ray of hope, dashed the following year when they shut down for good. By 1912, the Post Office had closed and scavengers were sacking the town. Inexorably, the elements began devouring what the vandals had declined to cart away.

Chloride and Mineral Park were but two of at least a dozen mining boomtowns that erupted in Mohave County. In 1899, a Kingman store owner, Henry Lovin, grubstaked José Jerez with $12.50 worth of supplies from Lovin's store. Jerez hit the jackpot when he struck a rich deposit of gold in the Black Mountains west of Kingman. Lovin named the place Goldroad, and he and Jerez sold the claims for $50,000. Lovin used his half of the money to enlarge his store, form a freighting company, and open a saloon in Goldroad. Jerez lived it up, squandering his $25,000 in a year or two. After a couple more years of mooching a few dollars in more grubstakes from Lovin, which produced no other finds, Jerez committed suicide by drinking rat poison. Sadly, this was a story often repeated throughout the West in those boom years, save, perhaps, for the dollop of rat poison. Adding to the irony of this episode, by 1906 Jerez's original discovery was worth $2 million.

Although Goldroad boomed for a time, the mine was beset with anxiety as the quality of the ore diminished and costs of production increased. The price of machinery, freight, and supplies rose significantly in the 1920s with no offsetting increase in the price of gold. The mine shut down, forcing many people to abandon the town. The few determined folk who chose to stay relied on a dwindling number of small operators who were barely breaking even. What remained of the community hung on desperately, even as the Great Depression set in. Compounding their problems was the fact that the economic slowdown diminished the traffic on historic Route 66, which ran through the center of Goldroad.

The country, reeling from the effects of the Great Depression, voted the conservative Herbert Hoover and an equally conservative Congress out of office and swept in Franklin D. Roosevelt and a Democratic Congress, ready to try anything to rescue the country from the crisis. One of the measures increased the price of gold from $21 to $35 an ounce. This measure resuscitated many of the gold mining communities in Arizona, as the U.S. Treasury now purchased newly mined gold for $35. This 60 percent increase in the price of gold, added to the deflation created by the Great Depression, proved a great boon to Mohave County, making unprofitable ore once again valuable. The idled mill in Goldroad was refurbished, the mine reopened, and people moved back. Once-moribund prospecting revived. There was even an uptick in travel along Route 66.

The good times came to an end with World War II. Mines in New Mexico, which produced metals infinitely more vital to the war effort than gold, had to be expanded; as a result, mining and mill equipment in Goldroad was commandeered. The town lingered, totally dependent on Route 66 traffic and a few diehard old timers convinced that someone would once again strike it rich. The final death knell sounded 50 years ago when Interstate 40 bypassed both Goldroad and its sister city, Oatman, by 30 miles. Within 20 years, the last vestige of the once booming mining camp had vanished.

When the U.S. government finally demonetized gold completely, allowing anyone to own it and its price to float, gold's value soared to a level that rekindled interest in gold mining. A limited operation was again opened in Goldroad by people commuting from Kingman. They appear to derive their income today as much from hosting tours of the old mine as from mining itself.

Three twisting miles of old Route 66 separate Oatman from Goldroad. This town, too, was discovered very late as far as mining is concerned in the Arizona Territory. According as much to folklore as fact, three years after José Jerez found gold in Goldroad, one Ben Taddock is said to have spotted flecks and small nuggets along a game trail in the vicinity of a great quartz pyramid called Elephant's Tooth. He staked a claim that he quickly peddled for a token sum to a couple of non-mining men from Kingman who resold it to the Vivian Mining Company in 1905. By 1907 the Vivian mine, in what is now Oatman, had produced almost $3 million and lent its name to the camp that had grown up near the mine.

The next year, another rich discovery developed into the Tom Reed Gold Mine. Soon, another high producer, the United Eastern, had sprung into production. Within the next decade, the Sunnyside, Gold Dust, Midnight, Snowball, Big Jim, Blue Ridge, and Lazy Boy were producing. As one would expect with all this activity, the population of the town had ballooned to nearly 10,000. Many did well catering to the needs of the people: Grocers, merchants, assayers, saloon-keepers, gamblers, freighters, blacksmiths, and ladies of the evening made good money. The majority of the men, however, worked underground hoping to strike another bonanza.

The increased cost of mining in the 1920s never hit Oatman with the force they inflicted on Goldroad, since the town's mines on average worked richer ore. Some continued to produce, though in diminished quantities. Others closed and the population shrank, but never to the extent that the town fell into desperate straits. When the Roosevelt administration raised the price of gold to $35 an ounce in the early 1930s, Oatman seemed revitalized. Mines and mills that had shut down began producing again, and citizens rejoiced. Then came World War II. Mine and mill machinery was shipped to New Mexico.

Postwar inflation caused all prices to jump—all but gold, whose price was fixed by the government. Most ore became impractical to mine. Even after the government stopped controlling the gold price and permitted individuals to hold gold again, only the exceptional mine produced ore of sufficient quality to make mining profitable. Most gold mined in the United States occurred as a by-product in the production of other metals such as copper. Adjusted for inflation, today the market price of gold would have to soar to around $400 an ounce to equal its 1935 price of $35. If mines were to reopen, Oatman's mining and milling machinery would have had to be replaced. The relatively low price of gold precluded this. Oatman's legendary mines never reopened and its population dwindled. Only the fact that some in the town could cater to travelers on old Route 66 saved the few citizens determined to hang on.

When Interstate 40 replaced old Route 66, all seemed lost. Oatman's population fell to less than 200 people before nostalgia intervened to save what remained—the legendary Mother Road that Okies used to escape the Dust Bowl of the 1930s. Thanks to novels such as John Steinbeck's *Grapes of Wrath* and songs such as "Route 66," Oatman's slow revival began. Heightened tourism has turned the town into a living (albeit fake) museum replete with curio stands and wandering donkeys. If the now long-dead residents of Oatman during its glory days could be revived, they would surely feel bewildered. Even Elephant's Tooth, the great natural monument that still dominates the landscape, would scarcely reassure them.

Yuma, circa 1890

This view looking south along the main street of Yuma reveals a good portion of the 1890s business district. With every blast of a locomotive's whistle, the railroads' arrival in the early 1880s sounded the death knell for Colorado River steamboat traffic. Although the Southern Pacific main line ran trains through Yuma, it never contributed as significantly to the town's economy as the Santa Fe did in northern Arizona communities. Cotton, citrus, and cattle have kept the town alive.

Times changed when Americans seeking to distance themselves from frigid Eastern climes discovered southern Arizona's mild winters. These fugitives from the cold, known as snowbirds, swell the winter population of Yuma and other communities along the Colorado River. To the surprise of longtime residents, many of these formerly seasonal visitors have come to stay. Retail shops followed the influx of newcomers—many of them affluent—dramatically transforming this old, dusty main street into a pedestrian shopping mall.

Yuma, circa 1892

A fleet of seven river steamers and five barges plied the Colorado River from the Gulf of California to the west end of the Grand Canyon, bringing to the western half of the Arizona Territory practically all its supplies. These steamers drew a very shallow draft, but it still required every bit of a captain's skill to avoid getting hung up on a sandbar. Vessels continued to operate for several years after the coming of the railroads. The newly completed Southern Pacific bridge appears in the background.

The Colorado River, which at one time made Yuma into a seaport of sorts, now is but a vestige of its former self. Upstream, a series of dams and canals diverts the bulk of the river's flow to other destinations in Arizona, Nevada, and California. Interest in preserving Yuma's historic landmarks developed only after many of them had been lost. This is true of the old boat dock, obliterated when the city built a parking lot. The railroad was rerouted years ago; it now crosses what remains of the Colorado at a new location.

Yuma, circa 1890

The Colorado River ran, albeit slowly, past Yuma in 1890. The current decreased appreciably as the river approached sea level, spreading the water's flow shallow and wide. Like locomotives, riverboats required copious amounts of water to make steam. Although water could be extracted from the river, it contained so much mud that it wreaked havoc on boilers. To solve this problem, boatmen installed a settling tank, the large structure with the conical roof seen in the historic image just beyond the bridge. Water was pumped into this tank and held there until the silt settled. The river steamers' tanks were then filled with the clear water.

A greatly diminished Colorado River dwindles in Yuma today, thanks to massive water withdrawal upstream. Large canals divert thousands of acre-feet of the river's flow into Nevada, California, and Arizona to satisfy municipal and agricultural water needs. The old railroad bridge was dismantled years ago and replaced a short distance downriver by a far more substantial railroad crossing. An elevated portion of Interstate 8 spans the river as the highway heads to California.

Yuma, circa 1909

The Yuma County Courthouse was built on the highest parcel of land in town. People at the time were convinced that the architecture of public buildings — especially those that housed the courts and official records — should reflect the inviolability of the law. Neoclassical architecture was deemed best at representing this quality. Even if a community could not muster the funds to build temples that would capture the glory of Rome, it could at least erect a building to reflect that grandeur to some degree. Sadly, this building was destroyed by fire in 1927.

The larger courthouse, erected in 1928 on the site of the old one, adjoins other county buildings. The Elks building, to the right of the courthouse in the old photo, was forced to make way for the complex. The latest courthouse reflects the transition from the neoclassical to the more utilitarian architecture of the 20th century, yet it maintains the flavor of the old building.

Yuma, 1900

Although the Quechan Indians managed to keep the Spaniards from colonizing their land for nearly two centuries, Americans intent on fulfilling Manifest Destiny eventually overran the area. Yuma first assumed significance for settlers during the California Gold Rush of 1849. It provided a convenient crossing point of the Colorado River for the forty-niners, who overwhelmed the Quechan Indians. After the Gold Rush, Yuma became one of the major settlements in the Arizona Territory, as it was an important starting point for miners intent on exploring what are now Yuma, La Paz, and Mohave Counties.

A Southern Pacific freight train rumbles past an elevated portion of Interstate 8 as both the railroad and the highway approach their respective bridges over what is left of the Colorado River. Yuma and the small communities to the south, Somerton and Gadsden, exist in the midst of one of the most productive agricultural areas in the Southwest. Winter vegetables and citrus fruits grown here grace tables across the country.

Ehrenberg, circa 1905

This community, first surveyed by Herman Christian Ehrenberg in 1863, was known as Mineral City. In the fall of 1866, after Herman Ehrenberg was killed in Las Palmas, California, Michael Goldwater (Barry Goldwater's grandfather) — who had opened a store in the town — saw to it that Mineral City was renamed Ehrenberg. It is likely that Ehrenberg looked much as it does in this photograph when Martha Summerhayes, the new wife of an Army lieutenant, saw it from the deck of a river steamboat. She was so disenchanted with its appearance that she refused to disembark (see Colorado River Settlements, p. 32).

The spot where this photograph was taken diverges from the old location by as much as 100 yards. Once river steamers were discontinued, it looked as though Ehrenberg might die, too, but a few determined souls hung on. The town managed a bit of a reprieve when a highway, crossing the river just south of Ehrenberg, was completed in the early 20th century, and it was further energized by the completion of Interstate 10. Visitors in their RVs now spend the mild winter months in Ehrenberg, fleeing before summer creates furnacelike temperatures.

Swansea, circa 1920

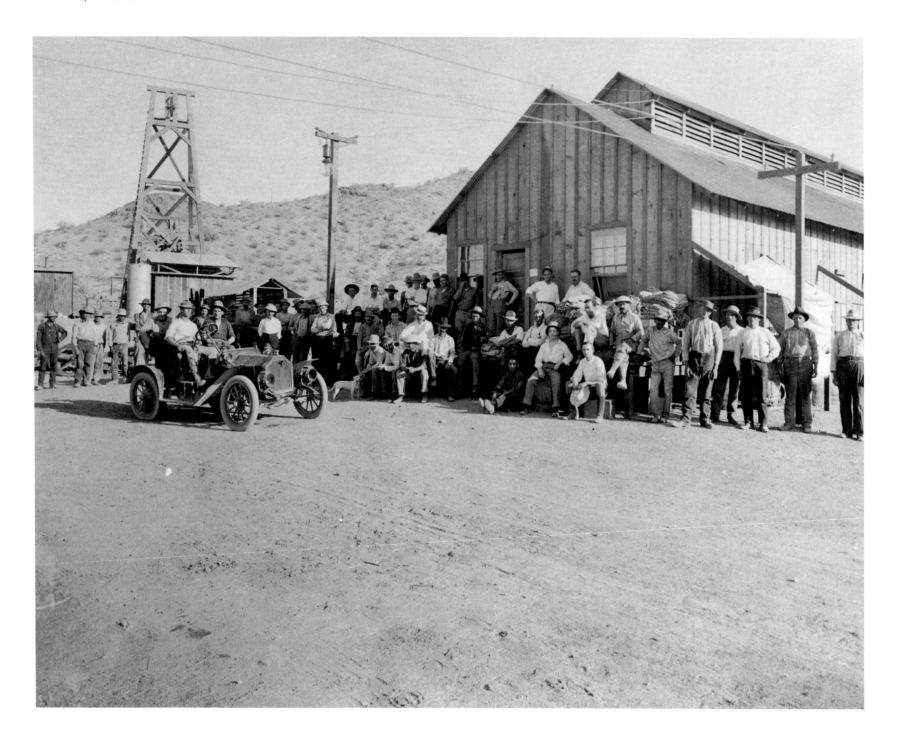

Swansea, Arizona, borrowed its name from Swansea, Wales. Prior to the early years of the 19th century, much of the copper ore from the Americas was shipped to Wales to be smelted. The workforce of Swansea, Arizona, mined an ore pocket tucked in one of the creases of the Buckskin Mountains. This photograph of about 50 men and a dog comes close to including all the workers at Swansea when the place was in full production. One of the most unusual aspects of this group is the appearance of several men who have defied tradition and doffed their hats.

There is little left to see in Swansea. The place was designated a historic site long after everything salvageable had been carted off and all but a few structures destroyed. Only the ghostly remains of a smelter, two units of a row of dormitories, and several concrete pads remain. The several deep shafts that once produced copper ore have been fenced off so the curious will not fall inside. Because Swansea is relatively remote and was developed late, it never generated the legends that many of the older and more colorful mining communities did. As a result, it beckons few tourists.

Parker, circa 1910

Parker never became a regular riverboat port, as no wagon roads connected it to the territory's interior. Parker only came into its own when the railroad finally laid tracks and built this bridge across the Colorado River in 1903. The locating engineer for the railroad was named Earl H. Parker, thus the town got his name. Note that when the picture was taken, the main channel of the Colorado passed under the far end of the bridge. After the next flood, it could easily have shifted. This variability meant that steamboat captains needed to be ever wary of getting stuck on sandbars.

The channel now flows permanently beneath the far end of the bridge because upstream dams now control floods. The river's course never wanders, and brush clogs most of the old riverbed. The road behind the chain-link fence lies just north of State Highway 62, which crosses the Colorado over a low bridge just downriver from this railroad bridge. Trains run infrequently, often days apart, as 18-wheelers haul most of the freight once carried by trains.

Ajo, circa 1880

Note the dark shadow at the bottom center of this photograph. It was not at all unusual for an early photographer to include his own shadow in the frame, as if to say, "I was here." Ajo is a Spanish contraction of the Papago Indian word au'auho, *meaning "paint." The Papagos used red copper ore for body paint, and when the Spaniards saw the paint they recognized it as a form of copper. The Indians disclosed its origin and the Spanish began mining operations. The first miners extracted the richest ore—which often included copper nuggets—heaped it onto burros, and transported it to the Gulf of California. There, they loaded it onto ships bound for Europe.*

The original settlement mysteriously burned to the ground. A week later, the first shovelful of ore from what would become the massive, open-pit Cornelia Mine was scooped from the place where Ajo had once stood. John C. Greenway, a wealthy engineer, was instrumental in building a railroad to connect Ajo with the Southern Pacific mainline at Gila Bend, enabling Phelps Dodge to ship its ore and bring in equipment. As the pit deepened, tracks were laid that spiraled down to where power shovels filled gondola cars and compact locomotives hauled them out. Since Phelps Dodge ceased operations in Ajo a couple of decades ago, blue-green, copper-laden water that the company once pumped out has accumulated in the bottom of the pit.

Clarkston/Rowood, circa 1915

Entrepreneur Sam Clark had no use for John C. Greenway's company town of Ajo, so he laid out a community he called Clarkston near the reduction works of the Cornelia Mine. By 1917, the town had about 1,000 residents. When citizens applied for a post office and proposed to rename the town Woodrow in honor of the wartime president, the Post Office Department refused the name. Defiant townsfolk transposed it to Rowood, which was accepted. Although overburden extracted from Ajo's open-pit mine threatened to bury the town, it hung on. But when a disastrous fire almost demolished the town in 1931, the town died.

Just beyond the shoulder of State Highway 85, once the main street of Clarkston/Rowood, faint remains of foundations and floors still linger. One of the great dumps from the Ajo pit is heaped up on the right. Despite the fact that mammoth dumps from Ajo continued to encroach upon the land on both sides of Clarkston/Rowood, the town's businesspeople refused to move to Ajo. Had it not been for the 1931 fire, the town might still be there. Today, many residents of Ajo express surprise upon seeing this photo pair, never having realized such a town existed.

Mineral Park, circa 1907

Mineral Park, on the west slope of the Cerbat Mountains, started as a typical Western boomtown, growing from a population of zero to nearly 2,000 within a couple of years. By 1907, it had fallen on hard times. (See Colorado River Settlements, p. 32, for the almost laughable machinations by which Mineral Park became the county seat.) Although several surviving bird's-eye views of the main part of town show the hotel, stage station, post office, and several businesses, such distant views do little to reveal the character of the houses and the people. What circumstance created the crowd at the far end of the row of houses in the photograph remains as much a mystery as the menu at the restaurant.

Judy Guerrero poses in front of the only remaining ruin in Mineral Park's row of houses. This tumbledown remnant is not the same house as the one seen at the far left of the 1907 photograph. Although this view is about 50 yards from the spot where the original picture was made, it does give the viewer the best sense of the town's decay and the desert's encroachment.

Chloride, circa 1914

The Fourth of July was one of the biggest events on Chloride's calendar. Men and women competed in street games together, one of few athletic events to involve both genders. The flags with six rows of eight stars indicate that this photo was taken after 1912, when Arizona became the 48th state.

Although this picture was not taken on the Fourth of July, it remains doubtful that a crowd even half the size of the one in the historic image on the opposite page could be convened. Chloride's population is far smaller than it was when all the mines were working. However, an American flag, now complete with 50 stars, still waves at the far left of the photo.

Chloride, circa 1905

The Cerbat Mountains rising behind the old railroad depot were home to nearly a dozen of the most productive gold and silver mines in the territory. These mountains produced enough wealth that the Santa Fe Railroad built a 12-mile branch from its main line at McConnico to Chloride. The gold strikes in Chloride and across Mohave County spawned the last true gold rush in the Lower 48. My mother and father honeymooned in Chloride in 1917.

The depot has sat empty for more than three quarters of a century and the tracks are long gone. Unlike many old mining towns with many empty buildings, one of the only abandoned buildings in Chloride is this depot. Recently, people from across the country have settled here, looking for a simpler life. A welcome absence of curio shops greets the visitor, as the town has not fallen victim to the peddlers of nostalgia.

Kingman, circa 1910

In this image, a mule skinner sits at the helm of a typical mule-drawn freighting outfit, ready to start on the two-day trip to Goldroad. Henry Lovin of the Lovin & Withers store grubstaked José Jerez $12.50 in supplies, and Jerez went on to discover the deposit of gold in Goldroad. It's quite likely that Henry Lovin would have used the profits from the sale of his half of the Goldroad mine to purchase this wagon team. The saloon next door closed when Prohibition was voted in with the 18th Amendment; it reopened with the repeal of that same amendment.

Motorists traveling on old Route 66 made a sharp turn at this corner of 4th Street and Andy Devine, a street named after the film actor, who grew up in Kingman. The Lovin & Withers building later became the Lang Theater, but it was abandoned when a new theater was built a block to the north in the mid-1930s. (The building shown in the old photo was later destroyed.) The famous road angled south at this corner and headed through Perfume Canyon on its way to California. The shallow canyon earned its satiric name because it served as a dumping site for raw sewage until a treatment plant cleared the air in the 1940s.

Kingman, circa 1910

Kingman, named after the railroad surveyor who laid out the route through Mohave County, owes its beginning to the arrival of the Atlantic and Pacific Railroad, which later became the Santa Fe. The railroad tracks enter from the left side of the photograph and continue past the center of the image before turning and ducking into a shallow canyon. In the days before grand sporting events, movies, and television, fraternal organizations played a central role in community life. These male lodges and their female auxiliaries determined most of a town's social interactions. When the Elks built a lodge here — the flat-roofed building at the photo's far right — it vied with the high school and courthouse for the title of Kingman's most substantial building.

The Elks Lodge appears in this view, though it is partially obscured by trees. Far more foreground is included in this image simply because Kingman has grown closer to the historic photographer's location. When Interstate 40 replaced old Route 66, which paralleled the railroad, the bulk of Kingman moved north to be near the new highway. A section of Interstate 40 can be seen as it cuts through the far hills in the upper section of the photograph.

Kingman, circa 1915

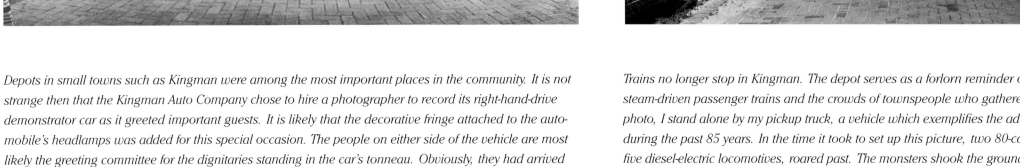

Depots in small towns such as Kingman were among the most important places in the community. It is not strange then that the Kingman Auto Company chose to hire a photographer to record its right-hand-drive demonstrator car as it greeted important guests. It is likely that the decorative fringe attached to the automobile's headlamps was added for this special occasion. The people on either side of the vehicle are most likely the greeting committee for the dignitaries standing in the car's tonneau. Obviously, they had arrived in Kingman via the Santa Fe Railroad.

Trains no longer stop in Kingman. The depot serves as a forlorn reminder of those glory days of the great, steam-driven passenger trains and the crowds of townspeople who gathered to witness their arrival. In this photo, I stand alone by my pickup truck, a vehicle which exemplifies the advances in automotive engineering during the past 85 years. In the time it took to set up this picture, two 80-car freight trains, each pulled by five diesel-electric locomotives, roared past. The monsters shook the ground, the pickup, and my confidence in my decision to park the vehicle so close to the main line.

Goldroad, circa 1915

In 1899, Henry Lovin grubstaked José Jerez with $12.50 in supplies from Lovin's Kingman store. This translates to no more than $200 in today's currency. The two sold their stake to the mine shown in the picture for $50,000. Jerez squandered his half and went broke by 1901. With his half, Lovin enlarged his store, bought a mule freighting company, and built a saloon in Goldroad. Although Lovin prospered, he did not fare nearly as well as the mine's new owners, who soon had a business worth $2 million.

By 1955, not a building remained in Goldroad. Unless a passerby was familiar with the former town, he or she would drive by it without notice. The road entering the upper left side of the photograph and continuing almost to the center before reversing is old Route 66. A lone mining operation in Goldroad now derives much of its income from hosting mine tours, which include cookouts, for groups of tourists.

Oatman, circa 1914

It seems an odd juxtaposition to see a 10-mule team hitched to tandem wagons in the same photograph with two Model T Fords. All wait in front of the United Eastern Mine headquarters. One is bound to ask, if gasoline-powered vehicles were available, why wasn't the mine using trucks instead of mules? The answer is that, in 1914, a team of 10 mules could haul a greater load than any truck of the era. The United Eastern produced more gold than almost any mine in the vicinity.

When the mines were closed and their machinery taken to New Mexico at the outset of World War II, it seemed Oatman might die, as had many mining camps throughout the West. Oatman held on. Again, its utter demise was predicted when Interstate 40 replaced the famous "Mother Road," Route 66, and bypassed Oatman by 20 miles. Despite all odds, a few citizens refused to budge. Because it was one of the few still-inhabited mining boomtowns, Oatman found itself with sufficient nostalgia to make it a must-see for visitors eager to experience the "authentic" West. Oatman has actually metamorphosed into a tourist attraction that original residents would scarcely recognize. Note the great landmark of Oatman, Elephant's Tooth, in the upper right-hand corner of the picture.

Oatman, circa 1925

This scene of the main street of Oatman must have been taken on a holiday, as it would otherwise be highly unusual for this many people to be on the street. Because of its vast mineral wealth, Oatman once boasted a population estimated to be near 10,000. By 1907, the famous Vivian Mine, obscured by the buildings on the right, had produced nearly $3 million in gold, and it was but one of a half-dozen fabulously rich diggings. The street in the picture eventually become part of the original Route 66.

One has to wonder how a street this size could have carried the traffic of one of the main highways in the country. Be assured, it did; and when it did, it never appeared as crowded as it is today. Oatman now is noted for its semi-wild burros that wander the main street, begging handouts from tourists. Like the one in the center of this picture, they seem quite content to stand for photographs for the hoards of visitors.

The settlement of Arizona and of the American West itself is inextricably linked to, and dependent upon, the development of railroads.

MINING AND RAILROADS

At one time, boys fantasized about becoming railroad engineers. They were ecstatic when an engineer so much as waved at them, and overwhelmed if he blew a short blast on the engine's whistle for them. Even had they realized that mule skinning called for far more talent, it would have made no difference. The raw power of a steam locomotive was awe-inspiring. Unlike today's diesel-electric locomotives, fully encased in sheet metal, those steam-hissing monsters displayed their mechanics. Ponderous, oil-glistening cam rods driving huge, counterbalanced wheels spelled out how this mechanical marvel actually worked. They shook the very ground. Compared to a 20-mule team hitched to a lumbering freight wagon, the iron horse came out ahead. A steam-powered train could haul a ton of freight for one-fifth the cost of a mule team.

So intense became the American infatuation with steam trains that people were willing to invest in almost any railroad proposal. Some unsound investments backed by con artists and overoptimistic developers notwithstanding, the public's faith in railroads never seemed to waver. But even at their height, steam locomotives were woefully inefficient, requiring copious infusions of water. They even harmed the very railbeds on which they lumbered. Steamers quickly wore out parts and were in a constant need of repair. Compared with modern diesel locomotives, they were extremely labor-intensive.

The early railroads that first crossed Arizona required small towns at regular intervals where the locomotives could water-up, secure maintenance, and take on a fresh load of fuel. As a result, the towns in northern Arizona came into being largely because of a railroad, rather than a railroad coming in response to their needs. Winslow, Holbrook, Seligman, and Kingman were founded as watering stops; all were named after railroad men.

The Bouse to Swansea Railroad is a case in point. In 1886, veins of copper were discovered by a couple of prospectors in what is now La Paz County. Because no railroad was nearby, the men determined there was no point in trying to mine the deposit, which languished for years. In 1904, construction of the Arizona & California Railroad (A&CRR) began. Its tracks would pass within 45 miles of the location. It was then that an eager metallurgist, George Mitchell, along with several others, realized that the mine's time had arrived. They acquired the site and organized the Santa Clara Gold and Copper Company. Investors gladly bought the company's stock on nothing more than a promise.

The A&CRR was completed by 1907 and Mitchell, a native of Swansea, Wales, began issuing stock in a proposed railroad that would link his mine, Swansea, to the A&CRR at the small town of Bouse. Investors bought eagerly, and a year later the first locomotive puffed its way from Bouse to Swansea. Mitchell spent investor money freely; how much of this ended up in his pocket is unclear. The fact remains, however, that the ore body was never extensive enough to warrant the large reverberatory he had built. What was mined by the Santa Clara Gold and Copper Company was shipped to the main line at Bouse and then on to Humboldt to be processed.

Unfortunately, the low price of copper did not cover the cost of smelting and freight. Mitchell relinquished his interest. With new management and the advent of higher copper prices thanks to World War I, the enterprise managed to eke out a modest profit. After the 1918 armistice, the drop in copper prices produced real hardship for the company. The Great Depression of the 1930s proved to be the last straw. By 1937, Swansea had become a ghost town.

Ajo was quite a different story. Although the mine there had to wait on the arrival of a railroad to become more than a small operation, Ajo was far older than Swansea. Its origins date to the 18th century. In Ajo, the copper ore was so concentrated that earlier miners could afford to load it on pack burros and take it to the upper regions of the Gulf of California. From there it could be shipped to Swansea, Wales, and sold for more than $300 a ton, or close to $6,000 in today's dollars — but such finds were rare. The development of large-scale mining at Ajo languished even after the Southern Pacific crossed southern Arizona in the early 1880s. Miners were eager to take advantage of the line's proximity, but none had sufficient capital or expertise to make a success of the operation until it was acquired in 1911 by John C. Greenway, a copper company engineer who had access to nearly unlimited capital.

Shortly after Greenway's acquisition of the operation, a mysterious fire swept through the few bedraggled shacks that comprised Ajo. The buildings occupied the land directly above a massive lode of low-grade ore that Greenway had determined to tap by digging an open pit. Ajo was in the midst of one of the driest expanses in the country, but Greenway drilled deep wells and tapped into a huge aquifer. He proceeded to build a railroad to connect his operation with the Southern Pacific at Gila Bend. Greenway then started digging a most ambitiously sized open pit, while at the same time constructing a mill and smelter.

Once his operation swung into full production, great power drills sank large-diameter holes that were then loaded with many pounds of explosives. A single blast loosened hundreds of tons of ore. Great shovels scooped up and deposited the ore into railroad cars. As the pit widened and deepened, the tracks constantly moved to keep pace with the shovels. Before the operation shut down in 1984, the awesome pit yawned large enough to accommodate an estimated 15 miles of railroad tracks.

Another great pit, which swallowed the entire town of Morenci, epitomizes the development and scale of copper mining in eastern Arizona. The Phelps Dodge operation in Morenci dwarfs even the Ajo pit. Extremely high-quality copper ore was mined by conventional methods in the late 1800s near the present site of Morenci. As the copper content of the ore diminished, Phelps Dodge chose to extract huge quantities of the lower-quality ore by developing an open-pit operation. In the intervening years, the company excavated a gargantuan pit and gouged 3.5 billion tons of rock from the sienna-stained mountains.

Copper was discovered in the area in the early 1700s by Spanish colonial prospectors in Mexico, but never exploited because of the isolated location and Indian threat. The site was unexplored until a lone prospector, Henry Clifton, happened upon it in 1864. He, like several others who followed him, also determined the place was too remote to become a major operation. After passing through the hands of several owners, the mines were acquired by the Detroit Copper Company, under whom the richest ore was extracted and mule freighted to the Southern Pacific Railroad at Lordsburg, New Mexico.

Until 1881, Phelps Dodge was strictly a Pennsylvania smelting business that processed nominal amounts of ore from several Arizona mines. The quality of some of the ore from Clifton so impressed Phelps Dodge management that they sent engineer Dr. James Douglas to Arizona to investigate. Upon his return, Douglas recommended that Phelps Dodge buy the Detroit Copper Company. One of the first things the new owners did was build a 36-inch narrow-gauge railroad to Lordsburg.

Once the operation was under way, Phelps Dodge determined to build a company town in a nearby valley, which it named Morenci. The management gave the planners of the new town great latitude, and they designed some of the most unusual and eclectic buildings in all of the territory. Fortunately, itinerant photographers hired by the company for the express purpose of photographing the town and its mining, milling, and smelting installations recorded much of the picturesque early settlement. Without these early photographs, we would never know the unique character of the town, as much of it now lies buried under a hundred feet of crushed overburden and the remainder has been consumed by the awesome pit. Municipal structures echoing the architecture of Prague, hotels vaguely reminiscent of ancient Crete, and even tennis courts have all yielded to the voracious maws of great shovels.

Nearby Clifton, the oldest copper town in Arizona, retains its turn-of-the-century architecture, though it is weathered. The mine buildings, the mill, and smelter are long gone. Without resorting to open-pit mining, the town produced close to a billion pounds of copper during its active life. Of all the mining towns in Arizona, Clifton—though never as opulent as the vanished Morenci—has

managed to retain a great deal of its original character. It remains one of the few communities still sufficiently remote that tourists and tourist shops have not overrun the town.

Jerome, on the other hand, epitomizes the transformation of a frontier mining town into a designated tourist stop, replete with all the trappings that characterize such places. Although discovered in 1583 by the Spanish explorer Antonio de Espejo, the town now known as Jerome, high above the Verde Valley on Mingus Mountain, sat unnoticed for almost 300 years. With the advent of a transcontinental railroad across northern Arizona in the early 1880s, the copper deposits on the eastern flank of Mingus Mountain, to the east of the Bradshaws, now assumed practical significance. Yet the cache of copper, which became known as the United Verde, languished until millionaire William Andrews Clark purchased the area. Finally the mine had the capital necessary to make it thrive.

The location of the ore body, directly beneath Mingus Mountain's steep eastern flank, dictated that the mine, mill, smelter, and town be built on a nearly 45-degree grade. Buildings barely one story high on the uphill side became nearly three stories on the downhill side, giving the appearance that the structures were poised to slide. The cramped nature of the location made the town especially susceptible to the United Verde smelter's sulfurous fumes. Regardless of the wind's direction, the town and nearby landscape seemed constantly stuck in its poisonous pall. After a few years of operation, smelter fumes will stunt or kill all vegetation they touch.

The United Verde bore the expense of shipping ore by wagon over a tortuous 60-mile road from Jerome to the Santa Fe main line until copper prices fell in 1891. Clark was forced either to close his operation or build a railroad. He constructed the United Verde and Pacific Railway, known as the "crookedest line in the world," to connect Jerome with Prescott. People joked that passengers in a rear car could look across curves and talk to the engineer.

Hardly had the railroad connected Jerome to the outside world when disaster struck. Fire started in one of the upper levels of the mine and could not be extinguished, making underground work too hazardous to continue. Unwilling to abandon his profitable enterprise, Clark realized that the only way to circumvent the fire was to switch to an open-pit operation.

Clark acquired the nearest flat area adjacent to Jerome and built a new smelter and a street of modest and identical company houses. The town of Clarkdale was born. The United Verde then dismantled the Jerome smelter and demolished the northern portion of town, where it started an open-pit mine. Within a few years, the giant rail-mounted steam shovel, like those used to dig the Panama Canal, tore out eight cubic yards of material with every bite. Soon the resulting pit had grown into a modern marvel. The excavation continued until the United Verde shut down its Jerome operation in 1953. When compared to the great pits at Ray, Ajo, and the mammoth dig at Morenci, it now appears modest indeed. But in its day it was without equal. Great, black slag dumps northeast of Clarkdale stand as mute testament to the extent of the operations of the new smelter that William A. Clark built.

With the discovery of gold and silver in the nearby Bradshaw Mountains in 1863, prospectors swarmed in. Precious metal was rumored to be everywhere and, strangely enough, it was true— mostly. Brigadier General James Carleton is often seen as the catalyst responsible for the region's success. In 1863, a prospector named Joseph Walker teamed up with Carleton and encouraged him to establish Fort Whipple to prevent the local Indians from interfering with the influx of prospectors. At this time, Prescott was nothing more than a collection of a dozen or so motley buildings some 30 miles to the west of Jerome. But Prescott's strategic location at the north end of the Bradshaw Mountains made it a hub for several extremely profitable mining operations including Joseph Walker's stake on Lynx Creek.

In the early days, the high cost of wagon freighting was tolerable given the wealth produced by the Bradshaws' many mines. Nearly half a million dollars worth of gold and silver were extracted every month. But without a railroad, Prescott's growth was far from stellar. The town depended heavily on a toll road, the Santa Maria, which ran to a steamboat landing on the Colorado River. The charge for the toll road was four cents a mile for wagons and two-and-a-half cents for a horse and rider.

Things changed with the completion in 1887 of the Arizona Central Railroad, which the Santa Fe (the former Atlantic and Pacific) built to connect Prescott to its main line at Seligman. The line was short-lived, replaced by the Santa Fe, Prescott and Phoenix Railway in 1895, but the railroad enabled Prescott to grow and the mines to prosper. During their active lives, the mines in the immediate area produced $2 billion worth of copper, and the value of gold and silver extracted from the Bradshaw Mountains is estimated to exceed $110 million.

With this rail connection to the outside world in place, and with so much wealth being produced, local entrepreneur Frank Murphy stepped in. Murphy had purchased the successful Poland gold mine southeast of Prescott. Like the majority of mine owners, Murphy grew increasingly critical of freight operators. Mule skinners—who possessed the now-lost skill of successfully maneuvering heavily laden freight wagons pulled by a dozen protesting mules over sharply twisting inclines—were not his favorite people. Certainly the prices they charged galled him. The obvious solution to his problem was a railroad. If he could build a standard-gauge line from Prescott to Mayer, he would at least save the price of 26 miles of mule freighting. In addition, his train could transport all the copper being mined in places other than Jerome to the new smelter at Humboldt. He completed the Prescott and Eastern Railway in 1898.

No sooner were Murphy's trains blowing smoke between Prescott and Mayer than he undertook construction of two branch lines. The shorter 8-mile line began at Mayer. It ran nearly flat for a way before threading its way up a fairly easy canyon grade to his mine in Poland. The long line he planned was a 25-mile run to Crown King. No one believed it could be built, as the tracks would have to raise a train 2,000 feet in elevation in less than 15 miles. The Bradshaw Mountain terrain was laced with deep gorges and near-vertical cliffs. Murphy's critics were convinced such a project was enough to daunt a major railroad like the Union Pacific, which had exhausted itself forging a way through the Sierra Nevada. When Murphy began construction, a host of local doubters dubbed his undertaking "Murphy's Impossible Railroad."

Taking three years to complete and going way over budget, Murphy's railroad proved to be a feat of engineering still admired today. The difficult terrain required five switchbacks, a tunnel, and several high trestles. By the time it reached Crown King, the town's best days had passed. Even so, the "Impossible Railroad" transported

Railroad switchback, Crown King, circa 1910

more than a million dollars in gold and silver from other mines in the area as well as the supplies they depended upon. The tracks were taken up in 1927.

Of all the copper towns in Arizona, Bisbee stands at the apex. In its glory days Bisbee supported a population of nearly 35,000. It all began in 1877 when an Army scout, John Dunn, found "color" (rich gold ore) as well as copper in rocks of Mule Gulch, a canyon in the Mule Mountains. Dunn staked claims but was unable to work them. He lost out to the man he had grubstaked, George Warren, who in turn lost them on a bet that he could outrun a horse in a 200-yard race. The winner of the bet lost them in turn, and the claims ended up in the hands of Edward Reilly, a Pennsylvania investor who purchased them for $15,000. Reilly then sold a 70 percent share to a group from San Francisco and together they formed the Copper Queen Mining Company.

The news of the fabulous ore got out, and soon the place swarmed with prospectors who filed a couple hundred claims in a matter of months. By 1880, a settlement of nearly 500 flourished. The ore was sufficiently rich to justify freighting it by wagon up to Benson, a small town on the Southern Pacific's main line. From there it was shipped to Phelps Dodge's Pennsylvania smelter. Here it came

to the notice of Dr. James Douglas, the same man who had turned down the purchase of the Jerome Mine and recommended that Phelps Dodge buy the mine in Clifton. It was obvious to Douglas that if the ore was rich enough to make this long haul profitable, it would be prudent to smelt it in Arizona and ship the finished metallic copper. Phelps Dodge made an offer to purchase the enterprise, but the owners insisted that the two companies be merged. The deal was struck.

By 1900, executives of Phelps Dodge were keenly aware that the company's smelter in Bisbee had become inadequate. The nearest adequate water supply—so necessary for a large smelter—was at Black Water, unfortunately located five miles south of the border. They did the next best thing and tapped into the underground White River just north of the border from Black Water and named the site after Dr. James Douglas. Wells were drilled, a new smelter was erected, and, as greater numbers of workers were employed, the town of Douglas grew into one of Arizona's important towns.

Bisbee also has a distinction few other mining communities can claim—a watershed labor event known as the Bisbee Deportation. Most miners, especially those from Eastern Europe, were well-known for demanding better conditions. Labor disputes in Bisbee came to a head in 1917. Unions, aware of the enormous profits the mining companies were making as a result of World War I, demanded higher wages and a 48-hour week. A minority of miners joined the International Workers of the World (IWW, or "the Wobblies"). The Wobblies contended that the war was between capitalists and was none of the workingman's business. To the less militant miners and citizens who supported the war out of a sense of patriotic duty, the Wobblies were considered enemies of the state. Talk of violence in promotion of a strike by the more militant miners—even those unaffiliated with the IWW—only added to the community's fears. The company-owned newspapers fanned the flames of anxiety and animosity. When a strike did occur, hatred and the whipped-up passions against the militants came to a head.

Vigilantes turned against their fellow workers, and with white kerchiefs tied around their arms and weapons in their hands, they rounded up the men they called German sympathizers and marched them to the ballpark south of Bisbee in the small town of Warren.

There, Major John Greenway addressed the "detainees," telling them that if they renounced the strike they could return to work. A little more than 800 strikers capitulated and were allowed to leave. The rest, more than 1,000 men, were loaded onto and locked into boxcars, and taken by train to Hermanas, a godforsaken place in the New Mexico desert. They were left there without food or water. Thankfully, Woodrow Wilson and the New Mexico authorities saw to it that food and water arrived in time to avoid fatalities. Phelps Dodge and the vigilantes in Bisbee scoffed, saying "those Commies got what was coming to them." When the news got out, most of the nation was horrified. In 1920, 200 of the vigilantes were tried and acquitted for the largest mass kidnapping in U.S. history. The jury foreman, J.O. Calhoun, proclaimed, "The verdict of the jury is a vindication of the deportation."

Beyond social fallout, the mining industry has left a physical legacy that marks Arizona's landscape. Huge, desiccated, abandoned tailing ponds abut US Highway 60 as the road enters Miami. The source of these man-made hills lies hundreds of feet below ground. Since the 1870s, miners in the vicinity have worked deep in the earth, blasting and prying loose rock, winching it to the surface, and grinding it into a beige powder. After extracting the copper, the remainder was run out onto flat ponds and allowed to evaporate. When it dried, another batch of tailings was added until today's artificial hills were built.

These hills did not begin in Miami until the early 1900s. Activity began there when "Black Jack" Newman, a native of Poland, was prospecting along Bloody Tanks Wash. Newman stumbled upon a great find. He named his diggings Mima, after his fiancée. About the same time James F. Gerald, working for a group of investors from Miami, Ohio, erected a custom mill near Black Jack's mine on Pinal Creek. In 1907, miners in the tiny settlement that had grown up around Black Jack's Mima Mine agreed to call the town "Miami."

The Inspiration Copper Company completed a new reduction plant in time to take full advantage of the demands that World War I put on copper production. The conflict boosted copper prices, and the Inspiration plant and the mines went into full production. The great tailing ponds that now flank US Highway 60 began to grow. Production after the war slowed but did not stop until well after the end of World War II. By that time, the tailing ponds had grown, taking on the dimension of the great hills that now rise above the town.

In the 1870s, after numerous encounters with the Apaches, prospectors succeeded in persuading the territorial governor to petition the U.S. Army to establish a post in the mineral-rich region of the Pinal Mountains. Camp Pinal did little to discourage the Indians, but did embolden prospectors and miners, enticed by gold and silver rather than copper. A soldier stationed at Camp Pinal had shown one prospector, Charles Mason, a chunk of black silver ore and told him the vicinity where he had found it. Mason had never thought it was worth pursuing and had almost forgotten the episode. Later his party reached a place a little east of Picketpost Mountain and encountered a small band of raiding Apaches. In the ensuing skirmish, one of the party, Bill Simpson, was killed and a mule escaped. When Mason found the mule, it was next to an outcropping of soft black rock that was similar to the sample the soldier had shown him some months before. Mason took samples of the ore to an assayer; to his delight, he found that it was as rich in silver as any ore ever found in the Arizona Territory. The Silver King Mine was born.

Mining ore at the Silver King was easy, but processing it was a problem. There simply was not enough water near the mine, though plenty of it flowed at Arnett Creek, about four miles to the southwest. The ore was so rich in silver that hauling it that far was worth it. Soon Mason and his partners built a smelter on a section of the creek, practically in the shadow of Picketpost Mountain. A small settlement grew up around the smelter, including a hotel and a stage station. The quality of the Silver King's ore slowly diminished, and the price of silver began to fall. Conditions continued to deteriorate. In 1888, the mine was closed; in less than a year the last inhabitant left Pinal.

But the area wasn't abandoned entirely. In 1890, the town of Globe, 13 miles west of Camp Pinal, was incorporated. Globe's development stagnated for lack of a railroad. All supplies had to be hauled in by mule freight from Silver City, New Mexico, 150 miles away. By 1880, a wagon road to Florence shortened the distance by nearly 100 miles, but things still languished. Globe needed a railroad. The community would have to wait nearly a score of years before the Gila Valley, Globe and Northern Railroad snaked along the San Simon Valley to at last reach their town.

Globe's Old Dominion Mine soon became the largest in the area. The operation included not just a smelter but its own railroad to Bowie, connecting there to the Southern Pacific. Old Dominion suffered from a persistent and seemingly uncontrollable flooding problem, which made deepening the mine impossible. The problems of the Old Dominion did not escape the attention of Dr. James Douglas. Douglas persuaded the owners of Phelps Dodge to acquire the mine. Antiquated pumps were refurbished or replaced; by 1905, the mine and smelter became truly profitable.

The economic depression of the early 1920s, plus the extraction of lower and lower quality ore, dictated the closure of the operation in 1924. Even so, the total output of gold, silver, and copper mined in Globe amounted to a whopping $134 million (approximately a quarter to a third of a billion in today's dollars). This helped to elevate the corporation, which had begun with a single custom smelter in Pennsylvania, into one of America's largest and most profitable mining enterprises.

The first hard blow of adversity for Arizona's railroad towns came with the demise of steam after World War II. Diesel locomotives proved infinitely more efficient, never requiring the vast amounts of water the steamers did. They were also far less destructive to the road bed. As a result they required fewer workers to operate and service and practically no track crews to maintain the rails. Great repair facilities in towns such as Winslow were closed, and all the towns along the Santa Fe felt the impact.

As automobiles became capable of driving long distances in the 1920s, US "Route 66" was established close to the successor of the Atlantic and Pacific, the Santa Fe Railroad. The towns along this route learned to accommodate the passenger car. Motels, cafes, and curio shops sprang up beside the new highway, and the towns prospered. A further jolt came when Interstate 40 replaced the legendary Route 66, as the new road bypassed established downtown areas that depended upon automobile-borne visitors.

Flagstaff, circa 1890

Because Flagstaff's nearly 7,000-foot elevation made the growing season short, farmers had to struggle to bring in crops before first frost. This valley northeast of the present city was farmed extensively early on, but the weather proved so uncertain that most farms were abandoned by 1925. Seen in the background are the majestic San Francisco Peaks, the loftiest mountains in the Arizona Territory, topping out at 12,633 feet. Since they were visible at a great distance from any direction, the peaks served as a guiding landmark for early travelers.

Though this does not appear to be the same location, we confirmed that it was by moving beyond the stand of trees to get a clear view of the peaks. Parts of the mountains can be seen on the extreme right. Businesses and this school have replaced the farms. Teachers graciously permitted a much longer recess so that the children could appear in the picture. It is heartening to see the resurgence of the ponderosa pine. Most of those stately trees were harvested by the turn of the 20th century.

Flagstaff, circa 1892

This bird's-eye view of the town was taken less than a decade after its founding in 1881. Notice the main street at the far right of the photograph. The Santa Fe tracks can be seen between the main street and the edge of the picture. The remnants of the ponderosa pine forest doting the town are a reminder of the huge uninterrupted stand of timber that convinced Edward E. Ayer to build the largest sawmill in the Southwest. Here, his mill furnished the ties and poles for the Atlantic and Pacific (which became the Santa Fe) as well as other Western railroads.

The Ayer Lumber Company, the economic engine of the community, was sold to the Riordan brothers. Under their stewardship, it continued to bulwark the economy for many years, but it has gradually lost its preeminence, replaced by Northern Arizona University and tourist industries. Notice that the patchwork of farms in the old photograph is absent in the new one. Flagstaff's elevation and subsequent frosts make it less than ideal for farming. Once the railroad was established, it was less expensive to bring produce to Flagstaff than to grow it there. The Santa Fe is now double tracked so that eastbound and westbound freight trains are separated. A daily average of 24 trains, each pulling up to 80 container cars, hardly slow down as they rumble through town.

The first wagon road to the Grand Canyon originated in Flagstaff, across from the Santa Fe depot. Most of the determined tourists arrived by train and stayed at this hotel, built in 1888. There they boarded a stage, like this one, that made its way almost due north to a point near the eastern end of the canyon, not far from what is now the Desert View Overlook. The roughly 75-mile route traversed relatively flat country, and the stage could usually complete the trip to the Canyon in three days. Two intermediate stations had to be maintained so that the teams could be changed and the intrepid tourists accommodated.

The hotel has seen several upgrades. Chief among these was the elimination of wood and coal stoves in each room. The chimneys remain, as seen on the right in the old photograph. The main street of old downtown (seen in this picture) was once a section of old Route 66. Flagstaff spilled over the original city limits years ago, but citizens have done an admirable job in revitalizing the old town center and preserving many of the historic structures.

Canyon Diablo, circa 1905

Canyon Diablo proved to be the greatest impediment that the old Atlantic and Pacific Railroad encountered in the Arizona Territory. Its construction stalled the railroad for more than six months while workers strove to complete the bridge. When trains began rumbling over the line, they would pause over the canyon to allow passengers to view inspiring sights next to the right of way. As this picture indicates, some travelers would alight and pose for the photographer, obviously a passenger himself.

This bridge, about 10 miles north of the abandoned settlement of Two Guns, is reached by one of the roughest rock and dirt roads in the state. The day this photograph was taken was the second attempt to locate the exact spot from which the old photograph was made. The goal was to photograph four to five diesel locomotives pulling an 80-car freight speeding over the massive bridge. As luck would have it, two derailments, one in Arizona and one in California, had stopped all trains.

Supposedly frontiersman Bill Williams christened the mountain named for him while trapping beavers in the area. Lumbering established the town of Williams below the lofty mountain. Later, the town was chosen by the Santa Fe Railroad as a departure point for a rail line to the Grand Canyon. When the railroad built this depot, it made sure to include a hotel and dining room, for in those days there was invariably a layover when changing trains. The initiation of rail service to the Grand Canyon made this natural wonder available to a far greater number of tourists.

With the completion of a serviceable highway connecting Route 66 to the Grand Canyon, tourists abandoned the train, preferring to drive. The Santa Fe ceased operation of the canyon line and closed its Williams depot. About 20 years ago, a group of investors became convinced that Grand Canyon visitors would welcome a chance to experience a bit of nostalgia. They acquired and refurbished vintage cars and two steam locomotives and began passenger service to the canyon. The project has been a spectacular success. Tourists park their cars and board the train for a two-hour ride to the Grand Canyon. Because parked trains obscure the old depot, I was forced to wait until their departure to get a picture of it.

Ash Fork, circa 1910

This was the famous Harvey House and Santa Fe Depot in Ash Fork. In the days when passenger trains had completely snared the public's fancy, the railroads spared no expense when it came to building grand depots. Ash Fork was no exception. In a town with a population of no more than 500, this depot was by far its grandest building. When a train stopped to allow the passengers to get a hot meal, every traveler could be served in the large dining room and lunch counter in a matter of 15 minutes. They would be back on the train in less than an hour.

The grand Harvey House remained in operation until the Santa Fe discontinued trains that did not include dining cars. After that it sat abandoned for several years until the railroad demolished it, primarily to reduce its tax bill. Today, even the premier passenger trains are but a faint memory. Now 80-car freights, composed mostly of flatcars stacked with huge container boxes and pulled by several diesel-electric locomotives, thunder through Ash Fork at the rate of at least one an hour.

Holbrook, circa 1897

The new Navajo County Courthouse was built after Holbrook had become the county seat. Navajo County had been carved out of Yavapai County in 1895, when local officials realized that it was no longer practical to maintain political connections given Holbrook's distance from Prescott. Notice the scrub covering the landscape. It provided very poor feed even for sheep and was an indication of the serious overgrazing that had taken place during the 1880s.

The chimneys on either side of the building are gone but the structure remains relatively unchanged. It no longer functions as the courthouse — the county complex has moved nearly a mile south of town, not far from one of the state's prisons — but is still a civic building. Settlements such as Holbrook fell on lean times when old Route 66, which went through the heart of the community, was abandoned. Tourist businesses, relocated north of the old town next to Interstate 40, are profitable and employ more residents than the railroad did.

Holbrook, 1902

Juan Padilla built the first house just east of Horsehead Crossing in 1871. In 1882, 2 miles to the east of the small community Padilla had started, railroad contractor John W. Young set up his headquarters. He named it Holbrook after the railroad man, H.R. Holbrook. This photograph shows wool being loaded. The perch from which this picture was taken, high as a second story, remains a mystery. Notice the man sitting on a sack of wool near the center of the picture and the scales next to him. He would weigh the wool and give the owner a chit for it, which the seller could then cash.

There is still a little activity at the Holbrook station, housed in the temporary building at right. Although this photograph was taken from the bed of my pickup, the camera is still at least 5 feet lower than the location the earlier photographer used. Note the size of the Santa Fe boxcar on the right side of the earlier photograph, and imagine an ordinary Kenworth 18-wheeler next to it. That truck's trailer capacity is greater than that of the boxcar, and it could have hauled all the sacks of wool shown in the old photo with room to spare.

Sedona, circa 1900

Sedona Schnebly lent her name to this community, one too small to warrant a post office until 1902. Sedona sits next to Oak Creek at a 4,400-foot elevation. Early ranchers found this picturesque red-rock area ideal for raising cattle. As with most ranches of the era, this one at Sedona was a Spartan affair. It was also remote enough to escape the attention of Eastern cattle entrepreneurs who created the large spreads that played havoc in the southern part of the territory.

When a pleasant year-round climate is combined with sublime scenery, it is safe to forecast that the place will act as a powerful magnet for the affluent who wish to get away from the grit and bustle of most large American cities. Sedona proved such a draw, and in the past 60 years it has grown from a few ranches (some of them dude), apple orchards, and mom-and-pop stores, into a gentrified sprawl. Fortunately, as in this picture, a smattering of the early Sedona survives as a sheltered island in the midst of explosive development.

Sedona, 1914

The photographer captured this romantic view of the red rocks of Sedona with the express intent to sell prints of this wonder spot. The number 533, in the lower right-hand corner of the print, is a dead giveaway. At the time, tinted postcards of grand scenery were the rage, and letter writing was the only way for people separated by any distance to remain in touch. Nearly all who traveled, and especially young women, bought such cards, wrote personal messages on the back, stuck on a two-cent stamp, and sent them to friends.

Sedona has been in a state of perpetual growth for so long that it seems a natural condition. The very affluent who move into the community acquire large lots and build spectacular homes. At first glance, this picture seems nearly devoid of houses, but a closer examination reveals partially obscured, upscale dwellings built on very large lots scattered over the landscape. One of the many homes perched along the top of this once-pristine vantage point precluded taking another picture at the exact spot where the original was exposed, but it is very close.

Oak Creek, 1915

Since the late 19ᵗʰ century, tinted postcards of the red-rock formations of lower Oak Creek whetted tourists' desire to see this special place. Although this scenic spot remained somewhat remote in the days of the horse and buggy, Oak Creek Canyon did lie on the main road from Phoenix to Flagstaff. Thus, it was far more accessible than Arizona's premier wonderland, the Grand Canyon. By 1910, tourists armed with the new, inexpensive box cameras could not resist the urge to snap pictures. Many, such as this one, survive.

Discerning viewers will immediately note that this photograph, although in line with the place from which the old image was taken, was made from a higher vantage point. In this instance, a choice had to be made. The "now" photograph could be taken from the exact distance, but houses would obscure the cliffs. Taken from a bit farther away, though, the picture not only reveals the red rocks, but also the new community of Oak Creek that all but fills the valley.

Jerome, circa 1919

This town was named after Eugene Jerome, who financed Arizona's territorial governor, Frederick Tritle, in 1886. Jerome's money enabled the good governor to buy the rich claim located on the eastern slope of Mingus Mountain from John Ruffner. Tritle sold out the same year to W.A. Clark, a senator from Montana. Although some large buildings can be seen on the lower slope at the left side of the picture, they represent just a segment—no more than half of Jerome. The rest of the town was built on the far side of the mountain behind the Montana Hotel, the large structure in the center of the photograph. This picture was taken shortly before the Montana burned in one of Jerome's most spectacular fires.

Today, Jerome still clings to the steep mountain, but many of the old buildings are gone. If you look closely, you can spot the foundation of the Montana Hotel. The background mountains in the early picture have been altered and in some instances obliterated by the open-pit mine. Note how the vegetation has regenerated since the closing of mining operations almost a half-century ago. Many people thought that, although the noxious smelter fumes had vanished, the land might never recover. Thankfully, they have been proven wrong.

Hell's Canyon, circa 1893

In 1893, building the bridge over Hell's Canyon was one of the major obstacles the Santa Fe Railroad encountered in its push to connect Prescott to Phoenix. Perhaps the most interesting thing to note in this picture is the boiler and smokestack on the railroad crane. We are so accustomed to the internal-combustion engines that power modern construction equipment that it is hard to imagine a time when steam did the job.

Amazingly, the old bridge still functions. It now supports much heavier track as well as today's diesel locomotives. The lower bridge, which at one time carried all highway traffic between Ash Fork and Prescott, has long been abandoned and its approaches destroyed. Note how the opportunistic junipers have proliferated, crowding out other native species that thrived before Arizona's rangeland was overgrazed. Their eradication in such rugged terrain is not considered practical.

Montezuma Castle is not an Aztec structure, as the name would imply. Rather, it was built by the Sinagua Indians between A.D. 1100 and 1400. Located on a great bend of the Verde River not far from old Camp Verde, it had become a tourist attraction by 1900. Note the formal dress of these picnickers: the women attired in long skirts and fine collars, the men in jackets fitted out with ties and cuff links. Note the soldier at the right of the picture wearing a cap very similar to those of Civil War Union troops. He faces a man sporting boots and a magnificent set of Burnsides, the side-whiskers General Burnsides popularized during that conflict.

These fragile ruins were designated Montezuma Castle National Monument in 1906. The Verde River has migrated almost a hundred yards to the south, and the old buggy trail has been replaced by a paved path. The cliff dwelling has been shorn up, some of the missing walls replaced and others plastered. A constant stream of visitors stays on the path and is no longer able to approach the cliff, yet the place still retains a compelling sense of the past.

Prescott, circa 1900

The story of how railroad builders brought the rails into Prescott is as fascinating as any tale of Arizona's territorial days. Nowhere is this saga better described than in Marshall Trimble's book, Arizona: A Cavalcade of History. This picture captures the opulence railroads lavished on depots in cities no larger than Prescott. It also shows the type of horsedrawn vehicles that awaited passengers. The few passengers, formally dressed men with valises, are a far cry from the diverse crowds seen today on any airport concourse.

The railroad tracks are long gone, pulled up decades ago. Eighteen-wheel trucks with name plates reading Freightliner, Peterbilt, and Kenworth now carry freight in and out of Prescott. A brokerage firm, a law office, and a hospice facility now occupy the old depot. The shopping malls on Prescott's outskirts, combined with the established businesses in the historic downtown district, seem to have left behind this depot, now a slightly out-of-the-way landmark.

Prescott, 1900

This bird's-eye view of Prescott from the turn of the 20th century reveals only about half the town. It had grown considerably since the first territorial governor of Arizona, John Goodwin, made it the territory's capital in 1864. Goodwin's decision, no doubt, hinged on the fact that he was destined to live in the capital, and Prescott was considerably cooler in the summer than Tucson, Phoenix, Yuma, or La Paz. The new courthouse — the large, light-colored building just to the right of center — was the showpiece of this still-modest community, which was stripped of the capital for the second and final time in 1889.

Prescott experienced a period of tremendous growth in the area between the courthouse, now nearly obscured by trees, and Granite Mountain, on the horizon left of center. Even greater suburban sprawl spreads for miles beyond the boundaries of the photograph, particularly in the area on the right. After being rated by major magazines as one of America's most desirable communities, Prescott has drawn even more people looking for an ideal place to retire.

Prescott, circa 1910

Many who could afford a horse and buggy were not disposed to giving a pair of horses the care and attention these animals required. Simply hitching and unhitching horses — the least of the requirements of ownership — were laborious chores. Walking and riding a trolley, for many, offered a welcome alternative. Looking at this view west along Gurley Street, one is struck by the 10 cross-arms on the telephone poles running along the north side of the street. In 1900, there were fewer than two telephones per 100 people in the United States — and none in Prescott. By 1910, the nationwide number had climbed to eight per hundred, and the poles along Gurley Street testify that residents of Prescott had joined the trend in the rest of the country.

The buggies, wagons, and trolley seen in the earlier photograph have given way to the automobile. Trees have matured, and telephone and power lines are now buried beneath the street. Despite these changes, downtown Prescott appears remarkably the same as it did 91 years ago. Stores have changed owners, but the new merchants have chosen to operate in many of the original buildings. Both visitors and residents believe this continuity makes Prescott unique as compared to most of Arizona's fast-growing towns.

Prescott, circa 1900

Prescott is one of only a few Arizona towns that has managed to retain a wealth of history amid fast growth, on account of the century-old buildings that still grace its downtown streets. This image of cattle near Thumb Butte, however, is a reminder of a formerly essential part of this vibrant community that has disappeared. These unlikely looking cattle once belonged to a local dairy.

Houses now fill the draw that once was a dairy yard. Thumb Butte Road has replaced the trail that led to the house and milking barn. Retirees gravitate to Prescott for its near-ideal climate.

Prescott, 1900

The settlement had been called Goodwin City, Granite, Gimletville, and Fleuryville. In 1864, it was finally named Prescott in honor of William Hickling Prescott, a prominent historian. These early, mostly wooden communities were prone to catching fire. With fire-fighting equipment so primitive, it was almost impossible to stop a fire once it started. This disastrous fire was started by a candle at 10:45 p.m. on July 14, 1900. It did not burn itself out until late the next day. In slightly less than 24 hours, a large portion of downtown Prescott lay in a great heap of ashes.

Prescott rebuilt after the fire; today, refurbished century-old buildings line Prescott's downtown. The community has grown so rapidly in the last few years that its downtown streets groan with traffic unimagined even 20 years ago. Although the townspeople would like to ameliorate the problem, they remain adamant that historic Prescott not fall victim to urban renewal.

Prescott, circa 1907

This photograph of Thumb Butte was made in accordance with a popular formula of the time—to include a straight road intending to deepen the scene by leading the viewer's eyes into the picture. It must have been taken by a photographer intent on producing a sylvan scene in country that, by its nature, seemed to defy his best efforts. It does, however, indicate the nature of the vegetation surrounding early Prescott that has since been overtaken by urbanization.

The primitive wagon road in the old photograph has grown into West Gurley Street. We may contemplate whether the crew-cab pickup with the camper shell, parked directly beyond the highway sign, will someday seem as dated as a covered wagon. The picture's recording of cars, trucks, a U-Haul store, gas station, and road signs, cannot but tell the future viewer of how wedded our generations are to the automobile.

Poland, circa 1907

In 1865, Davis Robert Poland located a mine that was to become one of the most productive digs in the Bradshaw Mountains. It was profitable enough to convince Frank Murphy to buy the mine and build a railroad from Mayer to Poland in 1898. Although a proper town never developed, it is possible to see the hotel, general store, and several rooming houses to the left of the railroad. Most miners lived in jerry-built houses within an easy walk to the mine.

The forest is back. The 19th-century mining operation forced owner Frank Murphy to harvest nearly all the timber in the vicinity. When his railroad reached the mine, however, it was possible to transport a much more carbon-dense fuel than wood. With the arrival of coal and the even more efficient coke, the remaining trees were spared. After the mine closed, the forest was left to regenerate itself. The land around Poland, save for the great, still-visible mining dumps, is one of the few spots in Arizona that appears much like it did before the arrival of Europeans.

Humboldt, circa 1907

Occasional heavy rains north of Humboldt could fill the nominally dry bed of the Agua Fria River in a matter of minutes and divide the town. At such times, smelter workers had to wade hip-deep water to get to work. The riverbed can be seen here between the old downtown and the hill. At their peak, Humboldt's smelters processed not only copper ore but a good deal of the gold and silver ore blasted out of the Bradshaw Mountains.

After mines and smelters ceased operation, those remaining in small Arizona communities such as Humboldt seemed marooned. Survival required most of their energies. Those who hung on had no reason to enact building codes and zoning restrictions; during the lean years, these were the least of their concerns. New residents eventually developed the enclave between the auto junkyard and the skyline. By the time these residents expressed an interest in zoning restrictions, however, "mixed use" had progressed too far in the old Humboldt to be reversed.

Crown King Railroad, circa 1910

This picture is of just one of the multiple cuts needed by Frank Murphy to complete his "Impossible Railroad" from Mayer up the Bradshaw Mountains to Crown King. Wiseacres were sure even a man with Frank Murphy's reputation for doing the impossible was doomed to fail this time. One stretch required 7 miles of track and a series of switchbacks to gain 3,000 feet of elevation — all to get a scant 3 miles nearer to Crown King. Although no accurate accounting remains, rumor has it that the railroad paid for itself before the mines in and around Crown King were forced to close because of diminishing gold content.

The railroad was dismantled a few years after the mines ceased operations. Because of the tenacity of a few hardy citizens of Crown King who refused to let their town die along with the railroad, county and state road authorities had to act. Highway engineers took advantage of the old railroad bed wherever possible and constructed new, sharply curving sections of road to replace several wood trestles and one short tunnel.

Crown King, circa 1907

The mine at Crown King vied for the title of the richest dig in the Bradshaw Mountains. Together, the Bradshaws mines produced legendary amounts of gold. So rich was the region that Frank Murphy was willing to construct his "Impossible Railroad" from Mayer to Crown King so the mines there would have access to the Santa Fe Railroad. Note the tiers of cordwood at the lower right of the photograph. Judging from their appearance, the logs are juniper and cedar. No doubt this use of the logs accounts for the barren aspect of the hills.

The foundations of the old Crown King mill are barely visible through a gap in the growth of new trees. Once trees around Crown King were no longer cut for fuel, they began a slow regeneration. The bit of road just to the left of the center of the photograph was originally the bed of Murphy's "Impossible Railroad."

In the short span of 130 years, the Phoenix metropolitan area has burgeoned from a sunbaked community of 240 into one of the top-10 population centers in the nation. In this brief interval, the original 360-acre townsite surveyed by William A. Hancock became a 3,000-square-mile sprawl. The original impetus for this growth lay with the U.S. Cavalry. Uncle Sam had determined that four companies of mounted troopers as well as one dismounted company were necessary to "pacify" the Indians of the Lower Verde Valley. Troops arrived in 1865, when Fort McDowell was established on the Lower Verde River.

Supplying such forts was a continuing and expensive problem for the Army, as the Cavalry was completely dependent upon animals that required far greater rations than did the soldiers. Not only did the Army have to feed Cavalry horses but also the mules that pulled artillery and equipment wagons. In those years, especially in Arizona, no hay or grain was cultivated locally. It had to be imported from as far away as Texas and Mexico. Post commanders throughout the West, under pressure to economize, encouraged residents whenever possible to supply locally grown animal fodder for the Cavalry. Exorbitant freighting costs of long-distance hauls could then be avoided. This "solution" presented another problem for Fort McDowell: In 1865, nearby civilians were entirely subsistence farmers, equipped to grow just enough food to feed themselves, let alone an entire Cavalry.

Probably in desperation, the post commander detailed some of his troops to clear and plant a few acres adjacent to the fort. Apparently, Cavalrymen did not make the best farmers. The yield of their farm was indeed scanty. A far better solution turned out to be the purchase of the wild hay that grew in profusion between Van Buren and the Salt River around 24th Street. Officials at the fort contracted with the few locals to harvest it. John Y.T. Smith, mindful of the Army's distress and his own need of funds, built a road of sorts over which he hauled the hay to the fort. This commerce was an early example of defense spending, which has since that time augmented the economy of Phoenix.

The patches where the wild fodder grew, which once fed the mounts of four Cavalry companies stationed at Fort McDowell, soon disappeared. By 1870, most of that land had been put to the plow and

PHOENIX AND VICINITY

transformed into irrigated farms. Irrigating the desert in 1870 was hardly an innovation. As early as A.D. 300, the Hohokam people had begun building an extensive system of canals to channel water from the Salt River to the area. By 1870, a new canal system, fashioned from remnants of the ancient one the Hohokam had constructed, allowed agriculture to begin to flourish again in the valley (see Ranching and Farming, p. 131).

The significance of the arrival of the Cavalry at Fort McDowell in 1865 is as hard to overstate as is the coming of Southern Pacific in 1887, the completion of Roosevelt Dam in 1911, and World Wars I and II. All sparked periods of growth reflected in census figures: 240 residents in 1870; 1,708 in 1880; 5,544 in 1900; 29,053 in 1920; 65,414 in 1940; and 106,818 in 1950. Less than 50 years later, Phoenix was rated the seventh most populous city in the nation: by 1996, the Census Bureau had recorded 1,159,014 residents.

Since World War II, the small-town character of Phoenix, which appealed to many servicemen stationed at nearby Army and Air Force training facilities, has vanished. Arizona's appeal for the ex-serviceman in the 1950s may have resembled that felt by a Cavalryman at Fort McDowell, who, after his enlistment was up, might have decided to make the village of Phoenix home. A Cavalry trooper could well have thought that by 1900, it had become too large and had lost the 1870s charm that once beguiled him.

Nineteenth-century citizens of Phoenix, especially merchants, were in need of a railroad. The entire community was at the mercy of mule freighters—a hard-bitten, irascible bunch. People waited expectantly for the Southern Pacific, which had arrived in Tucson in the early 1880s, to build a line to Phoenix. When the Southern Pacific began laying track, mule freighters and stagecoach drivers became especially surly, realizing that most of them would be driven out of

business. Faced with the arrival of the railroad, owners allowed their wagons and coaches to deteriorate. An already rough and dusty stagecoach trip to Tucson became steadily rougher.

Phoenicians had to cool their heels until 1887, when at last the spur from Tucson arrived. After waiting years for their railroad, citizens celebrated mightily when the first train rolled into town. The spur to Phoenix, which branched from the main line at Maricopa, propelled the town into a city of importance. Two years after the first train's arrival, the city replaced Prescott as the state's capital.

Had it not been for the development of the swamp (evaporative) cooler and later refrigeration, Phoenix summers might well have checked a great part of its growth after 1935. It is hard to imagine anyone today willing to endure a 110-degree August in Phoenix with nothing but a hand fan to ease his or her distress. Yet this was the reality at the turn of the century. Electricity was tardy in Arizona. Although George Westinghouse had succeeded in bringing alternating current to citizens in New York City by 1890, Phoenicians had to wait another 15 years before many even owned an electric fan.

Thanks to the foresight of William Hancock, who drew the original survey, Phoenix enjoyed an east-west, north-south grid of wide streets, instead of a crazy quilt of narrow lanes so common in older cities. These streets easily accommodated both wagon freight and carriages as well as horse-drawn street cars. Most citizens did not own a horse and buggy; they were a status symbol, not a necessity. The population of Phoenix in 1900 was slightly more than 5,500 and compact enough that almost everything lay within easy walking distance.

Nevertheless, people then, like people today, avoided walking when they could ride, even if it was but a few blocks. Streetcars charging a nickel were the answer. When legislators built the capitol nearly 20 blocks from the center of town, it was with the knowledge that they, at least, could ride the trolley from the Adams Hotel to the capitol. Phoenix was not the only town in Arizona to have trolley tracks. Tucson, Douglas, Bisbee, and Prescott all had them.

All citizens, including state senators and city fathers, were accustomed to Arizona's dust. Dust was considered inevitable, inescapable, and as natural to the place as cactus. The early pictures of Washington Street remind us that those early residents had to trudge through dust to cross the street or to board a streetcar. Even so, they were spared the stone-paved streets, befouled by horses, found in Eastern cities. The only experience in Arizona today that vaguely compares to the conditions of a noxious city street in Europe or America at the turn of the last century are the mule pit stops on the Grand Canyon's Bright Angel Trail. Upon visiting Phoenix in the early 1900s, an Easterner must have remarked how sweet it was to inhale no essence of stable, despite the dust.

True, gentlemen tipped their hats to ladies, greeted them politely, opened doors for them, and walked between them and the gutter lest they soil long skirts. These were the same gentlemen that denied women the right to vote, along with a whole array of other rights now taken for granted. Wives were expected to stay at home and cater almost exclusively to their husbands and children. The few free-spirited women who challenged the male-inflicted bounds were considered suffragettes and of low moral character.

Both men and women at the turn of the last century feared a host of devastating diseases. Those crippled by polio were a common sight. People died of "blood poisoning," a lethal bacterial infection resulting from something as simple as a blister on a heel. No child was spared bouts with measles, mumps, whooping cough, chicken pox, and, God forbid, diphtheria. Typhoid Mary (Mary Mallon) did not die until 1938. It was common to see vein-lined goiters hanging from necks, mouths sans teeth, emaciated consumptives, and individuals crippled or deformed by syphilis. Phoenix's hot, dry climate was considered especially curative for a number of respiratory ailments, especially tuberculosis. As a result, the town had more than its share of these sufferers in 1900.

The biggest fear in most cities in 1900, however, was fire. Wood was an easily accessible material, cheap, and beautiful, so most buildings were made of it. The danger that candles, lanterns, gaslights, and smoldering cigars posed on such flammable material was real. It goes without saying that the arid climate also made fire danger ever present.

Fire fighting in a town such as Phoenix might have consisted of a quickly enlisted bucket brigade that dipped water from the nearest horse trough until volunteer firemen could stoke a fire under the boiler of a steam-operated pumper. Once horses were harnessed and hitched, volunteer firemen hoped that, within the time it took to

Military Troops, Fort Verde, circa 1895

gallop to the fire, their engine would have enough steam pressure to operate its pump. Firemen also depended upon the hose team's arrival. The two-wheeled contraption that a six- to eight-man team pulled was fitted with a drum of spooled hose. All had to hope the conflagration occurred close enough to a fire plug that the hose could reach the blaze.

Under these technological constraints, once a building was afire it generally burned to the ground. If one in a block of adjoining wooden buildings ignited, the rest caught fire like a row of falling dominoes. So Phoenix endured its share of devastating fires. The original Adams Hotel, a Phoenix landmark and the town's most impressive building, was consumed in a spectacular fire in 1910. The lost marvel of wooden construction was replaced by another Adams Hotel made of brick, stone, and concrete on the same site. (It in turn

was destroyed almost 30 years ago—not by fire this time, but by implosion, to make way for the hotel that stands there today.)

Even after considering such conditions, most Americans have fantasized about existence during a simpler time. It strikes them when they feel irate over traffic congestion, the high cost of so many of life's necessities, and the seeming coarseness of contemporary culture. Would it have been more rewarding to have lived in the era of our great-grandparents? We often imagine that this time, perhaps the decade between 1900 and 1910, when most of the "then" pictures included in this book were taken, was idyllic. It's difficult to imagine how hard life must have been for most people at that time.

Phoenix, 1907

At the intersection of Washington Street and First Avenue (later Central Avenue) stood one of the most distinctive buildings in Phoenix, the B. Heyman Furniture Company. This scene reveals a bustling, now-vanished streetscape, including three crowded trolleys, three buggies, two bicycles, more than 60 men—and no women. The occasion for this apparent assembly is unclear.

The new buildings house the offices of large financial and legal corporations, which have supplanted the small, turn-of-the-century retail enterprises. Some will argue that the architecture visible in this photograph is at least as pleasing as that of the B. Heyman Furniture Company building. Architecture continues to reflect the values of the society that produced it.

Phoenix, circa 1900

The photographer set up his camera in front of the old courthouse for this view looking northeast to the intersection of Washington Street and First Avenue. Awnings on the building at left, and overhung porches on the hotel at right, bespeak the charm of the era. The hotel's prominent chimneys indicate that every room had either a fireplace or a stove. In those days, if guests wanted to keep the heat on, they had to tend the fire themselves.

This view, made for the original edition of Arizona Then and Now, *shows the dramatic transformation that transpired over three quarters of a century. Since 1981, the year the earlier book was published, even greater transformations have followed. Many viewers of these three images are struck by a sense of improbability that any contemporary viewer of the first or second image could have predicted the changes that were to follow by the time of the third.*

The 1975 Crowne Plaza Phoenix hotel, visible in the 1979 image just right of center behind the Newberry building, can still be seen through the tree branches between the high-rises on the right of the photograph. Many have decried the demolition of the beautiful historic structures of downtown Phoenix, contending that their replacements are sterile and impersonal. Others find the new architecture, although reflecting a style prevalent across the nation, to be as distinctive as were the buildings at the dawn of the 20th century.

Phoenix, 1905

The awnings and porches overhanging the sidewalk in front of businesses and hotels, seen here along the north side of Washington Street at First Avenue, remind us of the fact that citizens of Phoenix endured sweltering summers without swamp coolers or refrigeration. If shade did not keep direct sunlight out of interiors, temperatures inside might well have soared to better than 130 degrees. In the summer, hotel guests had their beds moved onto these balconies to take advantage of the 80-degree after-midnight temperatures.

No factor, except an abundant diverted-water supply, has been a greater catalyst for dynamic growth in Phoenix than air conditioning. The ability to air condition buildings influenced architecture in ways we scarcely acknowledge. Imagine a high-rise building that had to incorporate southern overhangs to shield interiors from the sun's radiant heat. Picture a Phoenix street or shopping center where awnings were necessary for the same reason. Imagine yourself living in summertime Phoenix sans air conditioning.

Phoenix, circa 1903

This view of the Adams Hotel at the corner of Adams Street and Central Avenue shows just how grand a structure this four-story hotel was. The one chimney indicates that the building was centrally heated in the winter. The lobby of the Adams was a favorite haunt of the territorial legislators. Much of the territory's business was conducted there. A few years after this photograph was made, the Adams burned to the ground in one of the greatest conflagrations Phoenix ever experienced, an incalculable loss for citizens at the time.

The foreground of this photograph was sacrificed in order to shift the view up so that all 15 stories of the latest hotel on the site, the Crowne Plaza Phoenix, would be visible. This choice provides a meaningful comparison with the original Adams Hotel. Less than 5,000 people lived in Phoenix at the time the early wooden structure was built; when this latest hotel was erected nearly three decades ago, Phoenix had at least 20 times the 1903 population. If the newer hotel had reflected this spike proportionally, it would have had to cover twice the area and rise 80 stories.

For the Boston Store at Second Avenue and Washington Street, a "dissolution sale" was far from a one-time event — rather more like an ongoing feature. The photograph is testimony to the fact that relatively few residents owned a horse and buggy when Phoenix was still a small town. Many who could afford one did not want the chore of taking care of horses. Instead, they chose to walk or ride the trolley that ran west along Washington Street to the capitol on 19th Avenue.

The trolleys that operated until the 1940s have been dismantled, a new city hall has replaced the Boston Store, and traffic lights now control the one-way traffic along Washington Street. Today, the only people you are likely to see riding bicycles here are the occasional team of uniformed city police who patrol the downtown area. A sign ordinance strictly regulates advertising — including that for modern-day clearance sales.

This Presbyterian church on the southwest corner of Central Avenue and Monroe was considered one of the grandest houses of worship in Phoenix. One can only speculate as to how much mud was tracked into the church. The appearance of the street surface leads me to believe that the photograph was taken not long after a rain.

Construction in downtown Phoenix languished throughout the Great Depression and World War II. Even the postwar pace of building in the city center seemed lethargic at best. The frantic pace of residential construction was never matched downtown until recently. Now most residents assume that the building housing a Subway restaurant and Michael's Jewelers will be demolished to make way for another high-rise. In a hundred years, will this photograph of the corner of Central and Monroe be seen with the same curiosity we now lavish on the old church?

Phoenix, circa 1905

Looking south along Central Avenue, one cannot help but notice the ornate building on the left side of the street. This is the original, elegant Adams Hotel, the meeting place of movers and shakers of the time. Before Phoenix was paved over, making it such a heat island, August nights here were a dozen or more degrees cooler than they are today. The graceful and commodious balconies accommodated guest beds during the summer months.

The building standing on the immediate left is a Phoenix landmark, the old Professional Building, once the tallest structure in the city. Just beyond it stands the 1975 Crowne Plaza Phoenix hotel. After the original Adams Hotel burned, it was replaced by a more fire-resistant model. This replacement also hosted VIPs until it was deemed too antiquated. The masonry structure was imploded to make way for the Crowne Plaza, the latest hotel on the same site.

Phoenix, circa 1905

This view of the intersection of First Avenue and Washington Street, taken from the top of the old courthouse, reveals Camelback Mountain.
The original Adams Hotel can be seen just beyond the beautiful building on the northeast corner of the intersection.

Due to a change in the roof of the courthouse, the exact angle of the original photograph could not be duplicated. The new camera position allowed me to include the recently completed Valley Bank Building at far left. The Crowne Plaza Phoenix hotel, which supplanted the replacement of the original, wooden Adams Hotel, dominates the middle of the photograph. The Deco-style Newberry store is the largest building in the foreground.

This current view of Washington Street and First Avenue shows that the Newberry store on the corner was sacrificed to make way for a parking garage topped by tennis courts. More high-rise buildings seem to be inevitable in a city growing at the pace of Phoenix.

Phoenix, circa 1914

This picture of horseless carriages parked on Washington between Second and Third Avenues includes, in all likelihood, all of the automobiles in Phoenix at the time. Autos were still a rarity and very expensive. Few could afford one; of those who could, only a few were willing to devote the constant attention owner-ship entailed. These early cars required perpetual lubrication of every major mechanical part. Then there was the kerosene for the tail and running lamps, and the acetylene generator for the gas headlamps. Even though tungsten-filament lamps would soon replace acetylene, the auto industry still had a long way to go.

City Hall, completed less than a decade ago, is a radical architectural departure from earlier civic buildings. Obviously, it's a far cry from the earliest wood and brick structures in terms of scale, materials, and concept. City Hall also stands in sharp contrast with boxy high-rises such as the Bank of America building seen in the upper right of the photograph.

Phoenix, circa 1900

In 1900, the population of Phoenix was 5,544 and the city's northern extremity ended short of McDowell Road. Although the Arizona Canal had begun delivering irrigation to the land south of Northern Avenue in 1887, much of the desert between Northern and Indian School Roads had yet to be reclaimed. North Central Avenue, beyond McDowell, remained a dirt road churned dusty by horses' hooves. Thus it produced plenty of material out of which even a small thermal eddy could fashion a fine dust devil. The Indian School had been built on the northeast corner of Indian School Road and Central Avenue because the land was considered too remote to ever have value for anything other than farming. Indians from reservations as far away as Utah were taken from their families and brought to the Indian School to learn English, among other subjects, and were taught to be "civilized."

As late as 1940, the city of Phoenix had not grown much beyond Virginia Avenue. When construction began on the Palms Theater, on Central just north of Virginia, many said the builders were mad to erect a theater that far out of town. By 1950, a few adventurous developers had risked carving small subdivisions out of the almost unbroken spread of citrus groves south of Glendale Avenue. Today, the only impediment to development along Central Avenue is Shaw Butte (seen in the center of the horizon). Had it not been incorporated into a mountain preserve, Shaw Butte would in all probability now be dotted with expensive homes.

Phoenix, circa 1910

Years ago, Camelback Mountain was Phoenix's mascot, its symbol of identity, even if it lay some miles northeast of town. Thanks to the proliferation of hand-tinted picture postcards, Americans everywhere recognized the mountain. Rearing majestically from the desert floor, the impressive mountain was second only to the Grand Canyon as the quintessential Arizona landmark.

Several decades ago, Phoenix had begun to sprawl out toward the base of Camelback Mountain. Luxury homes threatened to encroach upon the mountain itself. Fearful lest Camelback and its neighbor to the west, Squaw Peak, be overwhelmed, citizens demanded that both mountains be incorporated into a mountain preserve. Had it not been for their efforts and foresight, we might now see hundreds of ostentatious homes clinging to the mountain's flanks.

Phoenix, circa 1920

Ten miles northeast of Phoenix, a distinctive mountain juts above the flat desert landscape. Its outline reminded settlers of a kneeling camel, so it came to be known as Camelback Mountain. By the turn of the last century, so many postcards of the mountain had been sent across the country that people who had never been to Arizona were convinced that Phoenix must surely exist in the shadow of Camelback.

Cudia City, centered around 41st Place and Stanford Drive, was one of the first Phoenix subdivisions to encroach on desert land after World War II. Most of the building projects prior to this time had invaded either citrus groves or irrigated farmlands. Cudia City catered to buyers who longed to live in the desert, but not so far into it as to inconvenience them. Unlike in the massive new subdivisions now overwhelming the desert, early buyers in Cudia City strove to preserve the "feel" of the desert. Palm trees were planted, for didn't they belong in the desert? Never mind that palms were native not to the Southwest but to the Sahara.

This picture of the recently completed Arizona Canal, showing Camelback Mountain in the background, was taken from the hilltop upon which William Wrigley, Jr., of chewing gum fame, would build his mansion. In 1885, William J. Murphy undertook the job of building this 35-mile-long canal. The task required two years of concentrated effort by men and mules. The canal made it possible for farmers to establish citrus and date groves to within a half-mile of the southern flank of Camelback Mountain.

The western flank of Camelback was too elevated to receive water from the Arizona Canal, so it was never planted with citrus, but that did not preclude the later encroachment of buildings and homes. At the extreme left of this view is the eastern end of the Biltmore Hotel. Constructed at the apex of the popularity of Art Nouveau in the United States, The Biltmore has been refurbished several times and retains its prestigious reputation. The northern end of the Biltmore Estates dominates the rest of the scene.

Phoenix, 1920

Because of the quality of this farming snapshot, it is difficult to distinguish what sort of trees lie at the far end of the field, just south of the Arizona Canal. They may well be a row of young cottonwoods, and behind them a citrus grove. Early settlers in the valley planted cottonwoods along irrigation canals primarily as a source of firewood. Large branches were harvested from about a quarter of the trees each year. By the fifth year, the previously trimmed trees had grown new limbs large enough to be harvested again.

This area of Phoenix remained in agriculture until the early 1950s. Veterans taking advantage of the GI Bill's low-interest mortgage loans helped fuel the housing boom. Judging from the mature citrus trees growing in all the yards, the old hay field was converted into a grapefruit orchard not long after the "then" picture was taken. The expanding postwar population fueled the conversion of such groves into subdivision lots. These new residential yards often accommodated a dozen citrus trees.

North Scottsdale, circa 1920

This view of a typical small ranch seems to fall short of what Hollywood has led the public to believe about the nature and character of an Arizona ranch. Imagine trying to scratch a living from just such a place as this spot, west of the McDowell Mountains. The well-trampled ground shown here was not at all unusual. Cattle congregated around water, and if this was the only source of the precious liquid on the ranch, every head of stock was forced to come here for its daily fill-up. In the process, their hooves shattered the fragile soil.

The McDowell Mountains are not only the defining feature in many old photographs but also constitute a phenomenal sighting device. Their overlapping features allow a searcher to locate almost any object along a straight line. The distance from the McDowells, too, is easily determined with the use of a lens corresponding to the ones available to early nonprofessional photographers. As this "now" picture demonstrates, the phenomenal prosperity of Scottsdale has overwhelmed thousands of acres of the desert between Camelback and the McDowells. It seems but a matter of a few years until the city of Cave Creek merges with Scottsdale.

Scottsdale, circa 1920

Major Winfield Scott, an army chaplain, first saw the area in 1881 but did not take up land there until 1891. Five years later, the 70 residents of the community called Scottsdale had a post office. In this photograph, an unidentified family poses in front of their home. The indistinct line of trees behind the house likely comprises citrus owned by a family in one of the far houses. Cottonwoods behind the citrus border the Arizona Canal, which brought water to much of the arable land north of the Salt River. Although not evident in the photograph, in all likelihood this family either intended to farm or had already begun to farm a few acres.

This view represents some educated guesswork. From a vantage point where buildings did not obscure so much of Camelback Mountain, I was at the approximate location, assuming that the early photograph had been taken with an inexpensive camera that invariably used a "normal" lens. The key was to position the equipment at a distance that reproduced Camelback at a similar scale as the old photograph. A professional camera fitted with a "normal" focal-length lens allowed me to safely assume I was close to, if not exactly at, the original location.

Casa Grande, circa 1920

When the cattle craze hit Arizona in the late 1870s, the rich ranges on either side of the underground Santa Cruz River beckoned. By 1880, a major wagon road connected Tucson with Phoenix through Casa Grande, which became a major stagecoach and wagon stop. Soon, the Southern Pacific laid tracks through Casa Grande on its way to Maricopa, and the town began to grow. By 1920, rows of businesses and houses lined either side of the tracks. The Sanitary Meat Market, shown here, was typical.

Once the influence of the railroads waned, businesses abandoned train tracks and established themselves along the highway that traversed Casa Grande a few blocks to the north. Roads and automobiles sounded a tocsin for small-town hotels as they spawned a new phenomenon, the motor hotel, soon dubbed "motel." It is a safe bet that the Sanitary Meat Market either went out of business or moved north.

Casa Grande, circa 1920

Casa Grande began as a stage stop on the wagon road from Tucson to Phoenix. Although the Southern Pacific had arrived in the mid-1880s, its prosperity had to wait until the Coolidge Dam. The dam's promise of delivering irrigation water to Casa Grande was to remain a chimera; still, the advent of large irrigation pumps that could tap the Santa Cruz aquifer enabled farming to flourish.

The old depot is long gone, replaced by a structure with a plastered adobe look. As in other railroad towns, many of Casa Grande's commercial buildings that fronted the tracks have either been demolished or abandoned. The surviving ones have been remodeled, but the center of town has moved north. Despite the fact that Interstate 10 bypassed it by several miles, the town has endured and grown.

Tempe, circa 1900

This image is one of a pair made for a stereoscope viewer. This once-popular device produced a three-dimensional effect, and many scenic photographs were made especially for the stereoscope. Taken from the top of Tempe Butte looking northwest along the Salt River, this shot reveals just one railroad bridge. Charles Trumbull Hayden, father of longtime senator Carl Hayden, was a mule freighter who established a ferry and a flour mill just upriver from the bridge in 1861. During dry years like the one pictured here, the ferry would have seen little action.

Fenced towers on the altered summit of Tempe Butte have rendered the exact location unachievable. However, the resulting error is small, off by less than a dozen feet. The white structure to the left of center is the Hayden flour mill. To the right is Tempe Town Lake, impounded by a low dam in the normally dry Salt River.

Tempe, circa 1890

This view of Tempe, the community that grew up south of Charles Trumbull Hayden's mill and ferry, was taken from the summit of Hayden's Butte. Hayden came to Tucson in 1857. Four years later, he took up land where the oldest section of Tempe now stands and established a ferry to cross the Salt River. Darrell Duppa, the Englishman who gave Phoenix its name, is credited with changing the settlement's name from Hayden's Ferry to Tempe. A man steeped in the classics, Duppa borrowed the name from a valley in ancient Greece. The picture reveals a landscape reclaimed from the desert. The gabled building, situated in the midst of a citrus grove at the far left of the photograph and near the vertical center, is Old Main, the first and only building of the Territorial Normal School in Tempe, which later became Arizona State University.

Old Main is now dwarfed by many of the buildings of the Arizona State University campus, which has spread almost to the right edge of this "now" photograph. Should you be familiar with the ASU campus, try locating buildings and comparing their location with what is revealed by the old photograph.

Tempe, circa 1910

This image gives a good idea of the four blocks along Mill Avenue that constituted the business district in Tempe, originally a farming town like Phoenix. Note the sign, "BATHS 25," between the twin candy-striped poles left of center. These red-and-white poles identified barbershops for centuries. It was common for barbers to keep a bathtub in the back of their shops. The barber furnished a tub of hot water, soap, and towels, all for 25 cents. Often, men dressed in dirty and worn clothes would come in carrying new garments. After they bathed, they discarded the clothes they had worn in, and left togged out in the new ones.

The thoroughly urbanized Tempe is now the epitome of a college town. Arizona State University was founded as Territorial Normal School in Tempe in 1886 by the Thirteenth Territorial Legislature, called the "Thieving Thirteenth" (but that's another story). Such institutions were established to prepare young women to be schoolteachers. Prior to World War II, Tempe Normal School grew to be Arizona State Teachers College. A few years after the war, ASTC morphed again into Arizona State University. Today, the university's buildings have displaced most of the original homes that once existed east of Mill Avenue.

Apache Trail, circa 1917

Had the driver traveled from the Roosevelt Dam to this point—the last leg of the famous Apache Trail— without having to stop to change a tire or make a repair, he would have considered himself extremely fortunate. In 1910, it took a mule team three or more days to pull a heavily loaded freight wagon from Mesa up 45 winding miles to the dam site. All the laborers and most of the building materials had to be hauled to the Roosevelt Dam site along this road. Pictured is one of only a few straight sections, where the road passes a few miles to the west of Superstition Mountain. Until 1922, the Apache Trail remained the only road from Phoenix to Globe that did not have to pass through Florence.

Other than a section that is now paved, the road remains essentially unchanged. Those unused to mountain driving, who find themselves on one of the more precarious stretches of the Apache Trail, have been heard to mutter through clenched teeth, "If the highway people had the sense God gave a goose, they would have printed a bold red-letter warning on the road map."

In the 1880s, the route from Phoenix to Globe went southeast to Florence for 50 miles and took two or three days by horse. The trail then led north through Queen Canyon. When it emerged from the canyon, it turned east to Pinal. This 30-mile leg would so fatigue the horses that a fresh team would be necessary to make the last, tough, 15-mile leg to Globe. A quarter-century later, the construction of Roosevelt Dam was approved, and the first order of business was building a road to deliver materials to the site. Builders laid the road from Phoenix northeast to the dam site. The route negotiated some of the most broken country in the Arizona Territory. The result was the Apache Trail, which still can intimidate travelers unfamiliar with narrow mountainous roads. The long descent on Fish Creek Hill to the Fish Creek Bridge is particularly harrowing.

In its heyday, the Apache Trail was superior to the previous roundabout routes from Phoenix to Globe. It required only one day of travel by automobile—if the car did not break down. When the forerunner of State Highway 88 was finally built between Phoenix and Globe, there was no incentive to upgrade the Apache Trail, so it remains in much the same condition as in 1910. This replacement bridge is only marginally wider and more substantial than the original.

Roosevelt Dam, 1909

The 500-foot diversion tunnel dug in the cliff to route the Salt River around the construction site proved inadequate to handle the full flow of spring floods. Several times during construction, builders had to let excess water wash over part of the dam. The cableways across the canyon were held by fixed anchors that allowed the builders to deliver masonry blocks only directly below the cables. High on the right, a block of quarried stone is being ferried to the approximate location where it was needed. From there, it would be picked up by the adjustable pair of cranes and maneuvered into an exact position.

The heightened dam nearly doubles the storage of Roosevelt Lake, but this new capacity can only be used to control floods. Whenever an amount of water greater than the original capacity of the dam is impounded, it must be released slowly until Roosevelt Lake recedes back to its original capacity. Keeping the lake at no more than half capacity is intended to contain all future floods and spare the channel below the dam from river flows that can threaten or destroy the lower dams or bridges.

Granite Reef, circa 1907

In 1885, William J. Murphy dug the Arizona Canal, which started just below Granite Reef. A diversion dam—to make sure a reliable supply of water could be delivered to the canal's head-gates—had to wait more than 20 years. Granite Reef Dam was then built in conjunction with Roosevelt Dam. This encampment near the reef housed the dam builders. Everyone relied on horse-drawn transportation, so even Mesa, only 20 miles away from Granite Reef, was too far away for workers to commute to the job.

An abandoned gravel operation has replaced the workers' camp. A section of the Arizona Canal that delivers water to the Salt River Valley can be seen as it passes beneath a bridge just to the left of center of the photograph. The largely bare patch covering a portion of the high bank on the right is evidence of the beginning of the Central Arizona Canal's huge siphon tunnel. This massive underground pipe now channels Colorado River water beneath the bed of the Salt River, then up over the hills to the south, where it discharges its water into an open canal that delivers the water to Tucson.

Wickenburg, 1870

In 1865, Henry Wickenburg tapped into a fabulous deposit of gold in what soon became the Vulture Mine. His was not the only digging on or near the Hassayampa River. In those early days, miners had to haul gold ore to a small settlement on the banks of the Hassayampa named after Henry. There, a mule-powered stamping mill would pound the ore into powder so its gold could be separated, either by sluicing or mercury flotation. Eastern investors swindled Wickenburg out of his mine, and in 1905 he took his own life. As the mines around the town of Wickenburg began closing, the town seemed doomed. Area ranches didn't seem to be enough to keep the town going.

In the 1920s, wealthy Americans were taken by the notion that it would be a manly thing to play at being cowboys. Wickenburg ranchers discovered they could make more money catering to this pastime than they could by actually raising cattle. It wasn't long before their operations became known as "dude ranches." Such ranches around Wickenburg pulled the town back from the brink of extinction. Today, they continue to cater to the American cowboy myth while never subjecting their guests to any of the unpleasant realities of a cowhand's life.

Over thousands of years, the land and native species of Arizona fine tuned their symbiotic relationship, allowing both to prosper in normal years and to survive even in the hardest of times. Regardless of how resilient the range appeared, it existed in a delicate balance with the native grazing animals. The introduction of great numbers of foreign species, combined with overgrazing and adverse weather conditions, transformed much of this seemingly indestructible range into coarse powder. The newly denuded and pulverized soil, for the first time in its history, had lost the ability to withstand the forces of wind and weather.

Great expanses of Arizona are today home to cactus, grease-wood, desert broom, mesquite, and juniper. This was not always so. These are opportunistic plants that sprang up when animals cropped the grasses so short they could no longer crowd out the interlopers. At one time, the lands around Nogales, Douglas, Arivaca, Benson, Wilcox, Bowie, Tucson, and other communities south of the Gila appeared to beg ranchers to exploit them. And ranchers obliged.

Although the Spanish had introduced sheep and longhorn cattle into Arizona early on, cattle raising never became a colonial enterprise. Regardless of the many fanciful stories of huge herds of Spanish cattle and great haciendas, the actuality is far more modest. It is true that both Spain and Mexico made large land grants, but most of the successful ones remained in Chihuahua and Sonora, beyond the range of the Apaches. As Spaniards pushed north, conditions became more insalubrious. The Indian threat made any large-scale ranching a risky proposition. Occupants of early settlements such as Tubac raised just a few cattle and sheep and provided local Apaches with regular rations in a somewhat successful tamper to raiding. Even aside from the "Indian problem," there was no incentive to raise a large quantity of beef and mutton in such a sparsely populated territory with few markets. The few large ranches that did exist, mostly owned by wealthy Mexicans, were confined to the Santa Cruz Valley and south of the Gila River.

The U.S.–Mexican War and subsequent California Gold Rush were precursors of change. Food for miners became a critical consideration during the great migration into the relatively empty Golden State. The price of beef and mutton in California was 400 to 1,000 percent higher than it was in Texas, so ranchers from the Lone

RANCHING AND FARMING

Star State began driving their tough longhorns and rangy sheep across southern Arizona. At Yuma, they would cross the Colorado River and head west and ultimately north to feed the burgeoning populations. Their profits were handsome enough that they could afford to lose some of their animals to exhaustion, predators, and Indians in New Mexico and Arizona.

Many of those who drove cattle through the territory were impressed by the tremendous potential of Arizona's vast, now-vanished grasslands. However, in the early 1850s, the profit to be made in California was so immediate that the drovers could not take the time to develop new ranches in Arizona. They also realized that until Indian hostility was at least partially quelled, any large operation would be foolhardy. Things had to wait until Appomattox and the arrival of more than a token U.S. Cavalry before ranching could be extended into Indian territories.

By the early 1870s, the Army had succeeded in pacifying the Indians to a degree that made ranching possible throughout the territory. Many ranches were founded by Texans who had already seen the land or had heard reports by those earlier drovers; others had been lured by promoters. Within a few years, reports of their success snared the interest of Eastern money. Individuals with the means to finance large operations began moving in, bringing with them a better quality of livestock to replace the traditional longhorns.

By then there was a market for livestock in Arizona. The military became the biggest client of ranchers, in some years buying close to 1,000 head. The Cavalry depended on horses and mules, animals that demanded hay and oats, while the troops consumed corn, beans, beef, and mutton. So, incidentally, did miners. One of the inducements to persuade the Indians to agree to live on reservations was a regular government ration of staples, including meat. Railroad

construction crews had to be fed. With the coming of the railroads, mining in turn shifted into high gear, putting thousands of men to work. They, too, demanded meat.

Livestock mania spawned small Arizona communities where merchants catered to ranchers and cowboys. Often, communities initially established to serve miners were conveniently located in the midst of good ranchland, and the cattle craze spurred their growth. In great measure, these small communities reflected the character of the working men of the area: mule skinners, cowhands, black-smiths, barkeeps, and gamblers. Small entrepreneurs were quick to scout out a location, preferably next to a railroad or crossroad. There they would cobble together a general store, saloon, blacksmith shop, stage station, and a house where a red lantern could be hung over the doorway. These communities were as rough and ready as the mining camps.

Tombstone, for example, surrounded as it was by vast acres of rangeland, was one of many dual communities. The town was founded next to rich silver strikes that quickly became legendary. Later, the rough town was transformed by an influx of cattlemen. In that atmosphere, it was not unusual for Tombstone cattlemen to be as enterprising as the town's other businessmen. Most had close ties to saloons, gambling, and prostitution. It wasn't miners who shot it out at the OK Corral.

But like their counterparts in the mines, the cowboy's life attracted drifters, rootless men with no attachment to the community. A cowboy worked dawn to dusk at an occupation that, in all likelihood, left him crippled. Managing semi-wild 800- to 1,200-pound animals over a lifetime tended to take its toll. He endured all sorts of weather and unsanitary conditions, with little or no medical or dental care, for perhaps $30 a month and "found." Found consisted of bread, bacon, beans, coffee, and a cot in a shack, known as a bunkhouse. Most cowhands smoked dry tobacco known as "the makins," which they rolled into cigarettes themselves. (They were at least spared the serious damage to their lungs that plagued miners.) When they drank, they drank the same rotgut whisky the miners did.

In time, however, open range started to disappear; barbed wire was strung; riparian areas, springs, and seeps were fenced; and in most areas the small ranchers struggled to compete. What had once seemed endless grasslands had been sequestered in a space of 20 years. Unfortunately, little or no photographic record was made to verify range conditions prior to the massive degradation. Photographers working prior to the 1880s, when the overgrazing began, had little or no incentive to document range conditions. Even had they been prescient, there was no one around to hire them to do it. Photographs of pristine Arizona landscapes that would later be despoiled by overgrazing and clear-cut forestry are extremely rare, thus we are forced to rely on the journals and diaries of early travelers.

By 1883, the price of beef had more than doubled to nearly $35 per animal. Men infected with the cattle craze, rather than acknowledging the desecration their herds inflicted on the land, continued to import more cattle from as far away as the Atlantic Coast. As with all crazes, reason appeared to evaporate. Market forces ceased to be a limiting factor; only numbers mattered. Then, in 1885, a double whammy hammered the industry. Because of excess cattle, prices dropped by two-thirds, just as a vicious drought set in that wreaked havoc on an already deteriorating range. Desperate ranchers watched in dismay as their livestock began to perish. Frantic, they rushed to move starving cattle west to California, where the market was already glutted, and east to Kansas City, where sheer numbers overwhelmed the markets as well. The tide of cattle into Arizona suddenly reversed with a vengeance.

At the same time, the railroads jumped their rates. Sheep ranchers' experiences duplicated that of the cattlemen. They were caught holding gigantic flocks when the market contracted. The land around Holbrook and Winslow seemed ideal for sheep. The cold winter climate stimulated wool growth, and the summers, though hot, never approached the scorching temperatures farther to the south. Although the natural pasture might have been less productive than it was in other parts of the territory, with reasonable management there was the possibility that flocks and good range could coexist indefinitely. However, there simply was no agency at that time with the power to limit the number of animals on public lands. As a result, sheep ranchers increased their flocks until the ranges in the northern Arizona Territory were overwhelmed.

Given the opportunity, sheep will constantly move to fresh pasture, thus allowing the range to regenerate. It's quite a different story if they are kept in one place. Pound for pound, sheep that are confined to an area for too long are far more destructive on a range than cattle. Sheep have a tooth structure that enables them to take plants, roots and all, and their sharp hooves puncture dry soil that cattle merely depress. In addition, sheep are equipped to feed on a far greater variety of plants, and when kept on one range can, in a matter of months, destroy even hardy chaparral. When sheep are allowed to overgraze an area, they leave it as close to sterile as nature ever gets. So it was in Arizona.

When traveling to higher elevations in Arizona today, it is easy to be struck by the observation that there are a tremendous number of junipers and very little grass. How was this country capable of sustaining the vast herds that history reports? Originally the tall grass, which grew in profusion, shaded the ground, so opportunistic plants such as juniper found it difficult to proliferate. When an overabundance of sheep and cattle cropped the native grasses so short that they no longer shaded the soil, juniper seeds had a chance to take root. Within a few years, junipers became so ubiquitous that they shaded out the grasses.

The U.S. government was eventually persuaded to create an agency with the authority to help ranchers who failed to learn from the first disaster to avoid another such folly. If the conditions of the land have improved, however, it is largely due to the hard-earned realization by ranchers that the range is fragile, and that regulations imposed by the Bureau of Land Management (BLM), although sometimes onerous, are essential.

The heart of today's cattle industry no longer beats in the West. The majority of cattle are reared not on the range but in the enclosed pastures and feed lots of the Midwest. Steer, raised on feed laced with antibiotics, are brought to market never having had the experience of being at home on the range. The West is now a land where the most numerous "cowboys" are not cowhands with manure on their down-at-the-heel boots and battered, sweat-stained Stetsons on their heads. Instead, "urban cowboys" populate the area, shod in polished boots and topped by immaculate, imitation Stetsons. Now the Marlboro Man makes a good living selling cigarettes to consumers imbued with and seduced by the Western myth.

Stockyards and sugar-beet processing plant, Glendale, circa 1900

The history of farming in Arizona has even deeper roots than that of ranching. The valleys of the Gila, Verde, San Pedro, lower Colorado, and Santa Cruz Rivers, plus other minor streams, were farmed by various tribes long before the arrival of Europeans. In all of Arizona, however, the region along the Salt River just above its confluence with the Gila was historically the most conducive to extensive farming. An ancient and now vanished native people, the Hohokam, had by A.D. 300 begun an elaborate irrigation system that stretched for nearly 50 miles along the Salt. By A.D. 600, they were cultivating an estimated quarter-million acres, an area five times greater than industrious Anglos were cultivating in 1890.

By the time Europeans arrived, the Hohokam had vanished, leaving only scarcely discernible fragments of their vast agricultural system. The reasons for their abandonment baffled early researchers. Later, tree-ring analysis revealed that the nature of the Salt River played a pivotal role. Floods between 798 and 805 A.D. must have repeatedly damaged the sophisticated canal system. In 899, a monstrous deluge had to have inflicted nearly irreparable destruction on the centralized system, forcing a dispersion of many close-knit family groups. Scientists believe that succeeding periodic floods, coupled with intensive irrigation, raised the water table until it saturated the soil beneath even shallow-rooted plants. Lower areas might well have become bogs. This theory is not without support, as waterlogged areas again became a crisis for Arizona farmers, especially citrus growers, prior to mid-20th century. (Fortunately, by that time powerful electric pumps were operating on every section of agricultural land threatened by the rising groundwater table.)

In southern regions of what is now Arizona, 17th-century missionaries such as Father Eusebio Francisco Kino introduced the local Indians to the husbandry of European cattle and sheep and to the cultivation of grains. They taught Indians new farming techniques but, almost without exception, the Spanish and later the Mexicans did not hesitate to impose their own culture and eventually displace almost all Indian farmers. In the northern and eastern parts of the Arizona Territory, Indians (with the exception of the Hopis) rarely farmed even the riparian zones. The seminomadic Navajos, however, were quite amenable to sheep husbandry once the Spanish had introduced them to it.

Crawler/tractor and real-estate advertisement, Casa Grande, circa 1929

Tucson was a well-established Mexican village long before the first Anglos arrived there. Mexicans farmed a great many acres along the Santa Cruz River and ranched vast stretches surrounding Tucson. By the mid-19th century, only a few Indians continued to tend small plots between the town and the Santa Cruz River. A few others worked as farmhands for Mexicans. The most prominent business-people were natives of Mexico, and they controlled the majority of the wagon freight and raised more sheep and cattle than did the few Anglos living there during the years prior to the Civil War. The discovery of copper and the coming of the railroads changed things. In a space of 20 years, Anglos outnumbered Mexicans, and ethnic harmony began to evaporate.

Meanwhile, the establishment in 1865 of the U.S. Cavalry at Fort McDowell, in what is now the Phoenix area, created a strong demand for animal feed. Farming was undeveloped, so wild-hay cutting filled the need for a time, until mail contractor Jack Swilling recognized the faint remains of the ancient Hohokam irrigation canals. In 1867, he persuaded a group of Wickenburg miners to refurbish a portion of an old Hohokam canal. The locals dubbed his enterprise "Swilling's Ditch."

Frenchy Sawyer and Charles L. Adams were two of the first men to use the water from his ditch on a few acres that they farmed south of what is now Van Buren near 24th Street. It wasn't long before several more men were irrigating and harvesting hay, oats, barley, and pumpkins, which the Army purchased much to the satisfaction of the horse soldiers of Fort McDowell. Now their well-fueled steeds could hie them to the hinterlands, where they might meet and convince the Apaches that the U.S. brand on a horse's flank indicated the beast belonged to Uncle Sam and not to another Apache.

Mining at this time was especially labor-intensive. Without the muscle power of men, mules, and horses, the rich deposits of gold and silver of the Bradshaw District could not have been exploited. Miners there bought whatever produce the Army didn't, and the farmers thrived.

When Swilling's Ditch proved to be a moneymaker, more companies entered the canal business. As word got around that farming was more profitable than perhaps it ever had been, more farmers went to work clearing the brush from the ancient Hohokam fields. Soon, grain production had grown to the point that William Hellings formed a company and built a grist mill at what is now 30th Street and Fillmore. This enterprise and the pumpkin fields encouraged people to refer to the area as Mill City and Punkinsville.

A newly arrived Englishman, Darrel Duppa, accompanied Jack Swilling from Wickenburg to his operation in the Salt River Valley. Since Duppa spoke with an English accent, locals immediately dubbed him "Lord Duppa." Apparently Duppa could not abide such pedestrian names as Mill City and Punkinsville. Aware that this new community arose from the ashes of the Hohokam, Duppa, with his accustomed flair, maintained that the place should be christened Phoenix. Once the citizens were apprised of the name's significance, they judged it most appropriate and the name stuck.

By 1871, Swilling's Ditch delivered more than 200 cubic feet of water per second—enough to sustain 4,000 acres. Jack Swilling built a large adobe home on his farm, near today's 36th Street, which became known as Swilling's Castle. In spite of his contribution, Swilling turned out to be a great pain in the community's collective derrière. Though Swilling ended his life disgraced, his ditch had sparked other irrigation companies. By 1890, these were incorporated into a unified system that irrigated 50,000 acres.

The Salt River determined the destiny of Phoenix, which had come to rely on the river as surely as had the Hohokam. The Hohokam had implored deities to control periodic floods; Phoenicians importuned Washington, D.C., Congress appropriated money, and work began on the highest masonry dam in the world. With the completion of a nearly 300-foot-high structure that dammed the 1,000-foot gap

between the walls of a canyon far up the Salt River, the people of Phoenix were protected from the river's capriciousness. In 1911, citizens celebrated as President Theodore Roosevelt christened the dam that now bears his name. Not until the Salt River was tamed and its water impounded did people in Phoenix enjoy a truly stable agriculture.

Members of the Church of Jesus Christ of Latter-Day Saints, or Mormons, had originally settled the area next to the Great Salt Lake in an effort to free themselves from the religious persecution they endured in the Midwest. Mormons envisioned the spread of their apparently idyllic way of life, based on agriculture, over an ever-greater portion of the West. Church fathers therefore dispatched missionary settlers to colonize the land. Because they were farmers, the Mormons were ideally suited for the enterprise, as its first requirement was the ability to live off the land.

When Mormons entered the Arizona Territory in their quest to settle on arable land, they found few opportunities until they encountered the higher elevations of Little Colorado River. They acquired land from some earlier pioneers and, in a few years, they became the majority population in Snowflake, St. Johns, and Springerville.

Mormons who ventured farther south to the Gila River Valley fared even better. Many areas along that river were broad and flat enough to sustain large fields of irrigated row crops, and the Gila provided a dependable water supply. There they encountered C.M. Ritter, who had established the townsite of Safford in 1874. Joshua E. Bailey was already operating a small store. Mormons bought land and soon became the majority. They did the same in Thatcher, Pima, Solomonville, and Central. The U.S. Army had established Fort Grant in 1873 and Fort Thomas in 1876, and these installations went a long way in "containing" the Apaches, thus enabling the early settlers to expand their agriculture as well as their cattle operations.

Nine Mormon families under the leadership of Daniel W. Jones came to the area around what was to become Mesa in 1877. Things did not go well, and Philomen C. Merrill led a splinter group into Cochise County and founded St. David in 1877. Those who remained with Jones slowly made a go of a place they named Lehi, after a prophet in *The Book of Mormon.* Some of this group, along with new arrivals from Utah, took up land farther to the south and began

cultivation on a scale made possible by an irrigation system built on the remains of one developed centuries earlier by the Hohokam. This would become Mesa.

Mormon and non-Mormon farmers along the Salt River from Tempe to Buckeye were quick to embrace the opportunity to produce cash crops for sale to the Army and miners. At that time, animals powered all farming and transportation. By 1880, hundreds of miles of mule-freight roads had been established, and thousands of mules had to be fed. By 1885, the Army alone was purchasing tons of feed and hundreds of head of cattle annually.

Soon after farming had been established in the Salt River and lower Colorado River Valleys, a few farmers realized that one of the territory's greatest assets was the climate. It was one of the few places outside the Deep South and Texas with a long enough growing season to make the farming of cotton practical. Arizona had a distinct advantage over the South. Its extremely hot, dry weather rendered its cotton immune from the scourge of the boll weevil that regularly reduced the southern farmers' cotton harvest by more than half. Arizona was simply too dry for the weevil and too dry for mildew and rot.

The Salt River Valley, as well as the area around Yuma, proved nearly frost free, making citrus culture possible. The market for citrus was greater than either Florida or California could supply. Farmers soon recognized the opportunity and, within a few years, had planted thousands of acres of oranges and grapefruit. By 1910, great sections of the Salt River Valley had become one continuous citrus grove, while other areas were covered by a nearly seamless expanse of cotton fields.

Copper, cattle, and cotton interests—the "three Cs"—soon gained control of the legislature. Once they did, they were able to dictate policy for the state for nearly half a century. Until these industries were supplanted by other economic interests, such as electronics, manufacturing, and tourism, the governor and both houses of the legislature were largely controlled by the three Cs.

Payson, circa 1919

In 1882, Payson was known as "Green Valley" by the locals. When the small settlement was awarded a post office, the office and soon the town was renamed Payson in honor of the chairman of the Congressional Committee on Post Offices, Senator Louis Edward Payson. The valley, located below the Mogollon Rim, proved to be ideal ranching country — so good, in fact, that ranchers were willing to settle there even though Apaches remained a threat.

Until 40 years ago, Payson remained a quintessential frontier ranching town. Its rodeo was one of the oldest in the state and strictly a local affair. About this time, Phoenix promoters decided Payson was an ideal location for summer homes for those anxious to escape the summer heat. Today, that development, most of which has occurred north and east of the original town, has transformed Payson, making it a sprawling vacation community that old settlers view with a jaundiced eye.

Florence, 1894

Fourth Of July At Florence.

Even longtime Arizona residents are surprised to discover that Florence was, at this time, among the state's more important communities, as well as one thoroughly imbued with a Mexican tradition. When the legislature was passing out political plums, Florence possessed enough political muscle to enable it to wrest the territorial prison away from Yuma. In Florence, as in most American towns, Fourth of July parades were much-anticipated annual affairs, where nearly as many citizens were participants as spectators.

Although Florence remains the seat of Pinal County, the town has lost much of its former prominence to cities that have mushroomed since territorial days. This view of the street beyond the turning automobile points east in the direction of the state prison. The prison remains Florence's major industry, employing more people than either farming or retail businesses.

Florence, circa 1900

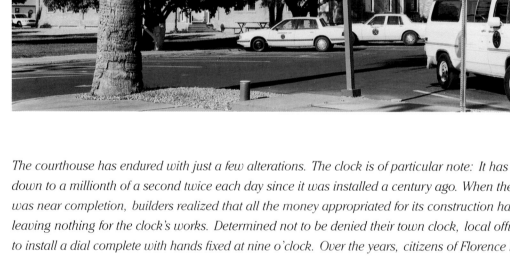

The Gila River emerged from the Tortilla Mountains into a broad plain. In 1866, an Indian agent named Levi Ruggles recognized the location's potential for agriculture and patented the land. Nine years later, he transferred title to the town of Florence. There is some dispute as to how the town got its name, but it is probable that Ruggles named it after one of his daughters. Early farmers were quick to take advantage of the moisture, and Florence soon became one of the territory's important towns, rivaling Phoenix and Tucson in the late 1800s. The opulence of the courthouse attests to the town's early prominence.

The courthouse has endured with just a few alterations. The clock is of particular note: It has been accurate down to a millionth of a second twice each day since it was installed a century ago. When the courthouse was near completion, builders realized that all the money appropriated for its construction had been spent, leaving nothing for the clock's works. Determined not to be denied their town clock, local officials decided to install a dial complete with hands fixed at nine o'clock. Over the years, citizens of Florence have become so attached to their nonfunctioning clock that they prefer to keep it that way.

Florence, circa 1904

This building, a blend of Sonoran and Anglo-American architecture, began as the county courthouse in 1878. By the 1880s, the community of Florence, settled mainly by Mexicans, had become one of the important communities of the Arizona Territory, ranking alongside Tucson, Phoenix, Yuma, and Prescott. When the courthouse moved to a larger building in 1891, this structure was converted into a hospital, and porches were added to provide some respite from the 115-degree summer heat. Without mineral wealth to sustain it, Florence's importance ebbed when the town was bypassed by the Southern Pacific. By 1900, Florence was deemed too unimportant to be counted among the territory's top 20 towns.

The hospital moved in 1938 and the building, now listed on the National Historic Register, housed several public agencies in the decades that followed. In 1974, Ernest W. "Mac" McFarland purchased the building and donated it to the Arizona State Parks Board. McFarland was the U.S. Senate's majority leader when he was upset by political upstart Barry Goldwater. He is the only man to have been the state's senator, governor, and a justice of the State Supreme Court, and he also owned the state's first television station, Channel 5. McFarland Historic Park is filled with relics and memorabilia from Arizona's history.

Globe, circa 1900

Mountains veined with silver and copper lured miners into Indian territory in the last half of the 19th century. Most of the prospecting activity centered around Globe, laid out by Alex Pendleton in 1878. The settlement was incorporated in 1880. Despite fanciful tales of wealth that spawned the fabled gold and silver camps in the Arizona Territory, copper has provided more wealth. Although copper deposits around Globe never rivaled the greatest found in the territory, they were still significant.

One of the grandest courthouses in all of rural Arizona can be seen just to the left of center in this photograph. Built in 1906, the structure reflects the prosperity of the city at the turn of the last century, when Globe's mines, including the famous Old Dominion, were producing millions of dollars worth of gold, silver, and copper. At that time, Globe vied with Phoenix as one of Arizona's most important towns. Now the building serves as the Cobre Valley Center for the Arts. Globe also houses the San Carlos Apache Nation Cultural Center; the San Carlos Indian Reservation lies just east of town.

Globe, circa 1912

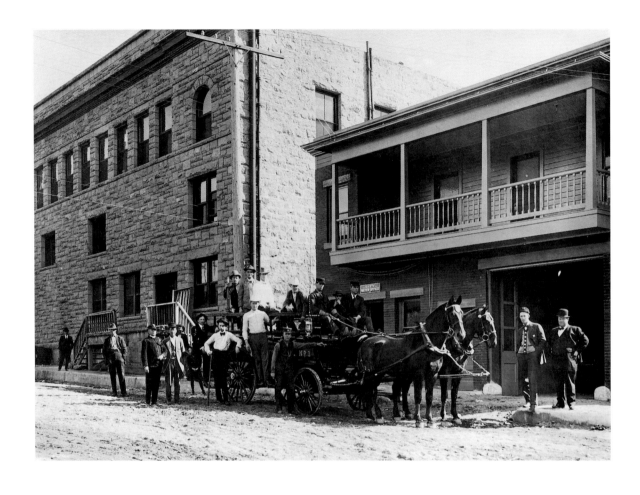

In this picture there are but four men in full uniform. These were probably the only paid firefighters. The others were most likely volunteers who would locate the smoke and then rush to the fire from wherever they happened to be when the alarm sounded. Fire was a constant threat to early communities. Once a fire started, it was extremely difficult to extinguish it using the equipment of the day.

Ninety years later, the same fire station is still in use, although it no longer has to share the building with the city water office. The department is very proud of its new engine, which the firefighters insisted be rolled out for the purpose of the picture. Now widened and paved, the street is one of the busiest in Globe. As a result, the camera had to be located a little distance behind the spot the early photographer had set up.

Central, circa 1905

Central was settled in 1882 by Mormons. Some say the town was named for the Central Canal on which the community depended to bring water from the Gila River to their farms. Contrarians theorize that the choice of the name simply referred to the town's location in the valley between Safford and Pima. Many find this image intriguing. People speculate as to what impending event encouraged these folks to line up along the railroad and even encroach on the tracks themselves. Was it their intent to stop a train which, in all likelihood, was scheduled to stop anyway?

This Central farmer drives his sand buggy much as other farmers do pickups. He was irrigating his nearby field when we asked him to be in the picture. He volunteered that he intended to race his buggy that weekend and that he would have to tune it to be competitive. Little else besides agriculture is evident in this area of the Gila River Valley. The old railroad track is a seldom-used branch of the Southern Pacific. Most business in the area transpires in Safford.

Solomonville, 1897

Solomon

William Munson built an adobe house at this location in 1873. Naturally, he named the tiny community that grew up around his house Munsonville. Three years later, he sold out to a German immigrant, Isador Elkan Solomon, who built a store and a charcoal oven. The community grew and became the county seat of Graham County in 1885. Although all the Apaches were living on the San Carlos and Fort Apache Indian Reservations, the U.S. Cavalry still kept a presence in most of the communities along the Gila. In this picture, we see troopers and Indian scouts at their noon meal. Things look pretty informal, including the soldiers' uniforms—nothing like the troopers in a John Ford Western.

Solomonville has now become Solomon, and many of the business enterprises have either closed or moved to Safford. These three children live in the small house at the far left of the picture. A couple from Safford are refurbishing the long-vacant building in the center of the photograph with the intention of opening a convenience market.

Eden, circa 1916

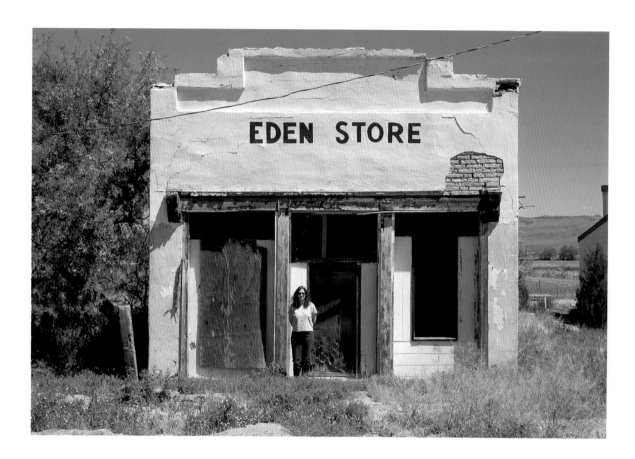

Lehi, Moses, and Moses M. Curtis left Brigham City on the Little Colorado River in 1881. They came down to Graham County where they founded a small community in the broad Gila Valley. Originally called Curtis, this small Mormon settlement a few miles west of Safford was later renamed Eden. The building in the photograph functioned as the community's general store and post office. Although we do not know who these people were, it is not hard to conjecture that the woman dressed in white and black belt and standing in the center of the doorway was the postmistress and wife of the proprietor.

Wendy Dutton now stands in the doorway of the long-abandoned building. At the right, fields can be glimpsed, and beyond them the Gila River. The Gila Mountains separate the San Carlos Indian Reservation from the Gila Valley. As in so many small Arizona communities, the mom-and-pop store in Eden is a thing of the past. Now the farmers around Eden drive to nearby Pima and Safford to shop.

Duncan, circa 1915

In 1883 — a scant two years after they sold the land on which this town now sits to the New Mexico Railroad — brothers Guthrie and J. Duncan Smith were killed by Apaches. This railroad connected Clifton to the Southern Pacific main line, and the small station built there was named after brother Duncan. At 3,878 feet above sea level, Duncan sat higher than any other Arizona farming community on the Gila River with the exception of its neighbor, Franklin. Only 20 miles south of Clifton, Duncan was ideally located to sell crops to the mines.

A combination of events has left Duncan greatly diminished. This unique old drug and jewelry store, built with salvaged concrete railroad ties, has long sat abandoned, just as do many of the once-flourishing stores in town. Duncan's small businesses have suffered the fate of those in many small Arizona communities within easy driving distance of bigger towns and larger stores. In Duncan's case, that town is Safford.

Springerville, circa 1924

During the last half of the 19ᵗʰ century, Mormon settlers followed the Little Colorado River to a broad plain nestled at the north end of an impressive range of mountains. There they commenced farming. An enterprising man named Becker founded a general merchandise store — the nearest thing to an emporium in that section of the territory. He sold everything from general dry goods to wagons and plows.

The grand Becker store has been replaced by a McDonald's, pickups have replaced the old touring cars, and all the streets are now paved, yet Springerville still retains many of the characteristics of the original community. The town sits at the north end of a vast vacation area that draws thousands of visitors fleeing the summer heat of Phoenix.

Morenci, 1900–1916

The minerals at Morenci were discovered by the Metcalf brothers when they were working as Army scouts in 1872. The brothers sold their interest in the claims to Charles and Henry Lesinsky of Las Cruces, New Mexico. In 1881, the Lesinskys joined with Captain Miles Joy to form the Detroit Copper Company, which sold out to Phelps Dodge in 1885 for $2 million. After making a major investment that enlarged the operation, Phelps Dodge began to mine copper ore at an ever-increasing rate. The company's expanding operations required so many workers that Morenci grew into one of the Arizona Territory's largest and most elegant mining towns. Phelps Dodge Corporation extracted a record 3.5 billion tons of copper-bearing rock—but in the process, leveled the town.

Morenci commands our attention because of its historic interest and the scale of its destruction. Large mining companies did have a habit of devouring towns as they expanded operations. Ajo mysteriously burnt to the ground prior to the digging of the great pit that removed the ground upon which it was built; still, Ajo was just a small collection of decrepit buildings. The communities of Ray and Sonora, though both larger than the original Ajo, amounted to perhaps two dozen buildings and a few shacks when they gave way to the great pit still mined today. The northern section of Jerome also succumbed to the steam shovel; happily, the southern half of the town survived. By 1910, Morenci was nearly as populous as Bisbee, and larger than Jerome. Images of historic Morenci record some of the most unique architecture in the Arizona Territory. No one at the time could have conceived that such an important town was destined to be as ephemeral as a cloud.

The content of copper in the ore beneath Ajo, Bisbee, Clifton, Miami, Globe, Swansea, and Mineral Park steadily declined, and with it mining activity. Morenci, on the other hand, suffered the fortune (and misfortune) of sitting atop one of America's greatest deposits of profitable copper ore, at a time when mining machines were growing far larger and more efficient. Thus the original town of Morenci, the hills upon which it was built, and the ground upon which the old photographers had set up their cameras, all fell victim to the insatiable maws of gargantuan shovels. It is now impossible to position a camera on the same ground where the early photographers had placed theirs. *Arizona Then and Now* would be greatly diminished, however, should Morenci be excluded on the grounds that its inclusion would be at variance with the format of the book.

Morenci, circa 1900

This is a view of part of the town that grew up around the mine. It is interesting to pick out and trace the railroad tracks from the one that enters the picture at the upper right to the four sets that dominate the center of the photograph. The lower tracks lead to twin rectangular caches of cordwood. Wood, at this time, was the fuel powering the mining machines in Morenci.

circa 1904

This overlook encompasses the principal mining operations. The ore dumps that dominate the lower section of the photograph are an indication of its scope. The company's operation can be seen at the center of the photograph. When this image is compared with the photo at left, it is evident that the mining enterprise has enlarged dramatically. Note the expansion of the railroad and the tailings from test-tunnels in the hillsides. These were dug to ascertain the extent of the ore deposits there.

circa 1907

circa 1910

circa 1916

What a grand, eclectic example of territorial architecture. Note the Gila Valley Bank and Trust office on the lower floor to the left of the entrance and the post office at its right. Apparently the three-seat surreys discharged guests at the spot where they are parked, leaving visitors to ascend the long set of stairs leading to the grand entrance. The two ornate chimneys suggest that the building had central heat at a time when most hotels in the Arizona Territory had stoves in every room. We are left to speculate as to the purpose of the louvered structure with the tall smokestack at the far right of the picture.

By 1910, exploratory work evidently convinced Phelps Dodge that the mine could tap one of the greatest bodies of copper ore in the entire nation. Mining had been expanded on the far hillside as well as in the area at the bottom right of the photograph. The three grand buildings in this photo are evidence of the town's new stature. Still, we wonder why the fancy hotel in the center of the photograph was built on the dump. We can only guess at the purpose of the long set of steps descending from the hotel's porch, which seem to lead to nowhere.

This view reveals most of the company's processing plant. It is obvious that the bulk of mining was performed in areas beyond the boundaries of this picture. The single-hoist frame breaking the center of the horizon would have been totally incapable of bringing enough ore to the surface to feed this large an operation. Notice the two men walking along the road in the lower right. They provide a much-needed scale to enable the viewer to realize just how large this processing plant was, destined to vanish along with the entire town.

Morenci, circa 1910

This image conveys some sense of the workers' living accommodations. The railroad trestle, seen at the lower left of the photograph, was constructed prior to the advent of modern trucks capable of hauling multiple tons of ore. Transportation of huge loads depended upon railroads. Without them the mines had to rely on mule freight at a cost four to five times as much per ton of ore.

The spot from which the previous image was taken has fallen victim to the mine's operations. However, this view was made from a vantage point no more than 200 feet from the original. Regardless of the discrepancy, the pair gives the viewer a sense of the ordinary homes that once clung to the hillsides, along with their fairly recent replacements. These newer houses have been boarded up pending their removal to make room for the further enlargement of the mine.

The Morenci Pit

Visible on the far side of the Morenci Pit operation are the more recent and far broader terraces, able to support today's huge machinery. The ore trucks, which look tiny in the photograph, are actually some of the largest commercial vehicles manufactured. The undersides of these gigantic haulers loom far enough above the ground that a compact car could drive underneath one. Follow the behemoth trucks that bear loads from two locations. These areas, however, are obscured by sections of terraced hillsides, one on the extreme left and the other left of center of the left section of the photograph. Trucks are visible at right dumping their loads over the edge of the 20-foot-deep fill, which sits atop another such fill, which in turn rests upon another, and yet another. Mining goes on 24 hours a day.

This gigantic enterprise gouged 3.5 billion tons of copper-bearing ore from the earth. Perhaps the operation should not be considered a true pit, since the prodigious tonnage of ore has been torn from the hills flanking Chase Creek. The deepest areas of the "pit" are continually being filled by overburden, a low-grade ore not worth processing. Overburden, as the name implies, must be removed to access the much richer ore lying beneath it. The repositories of this valuable ore — hillsides — are peeled away by giant shovels that operate along the terraces. Note the abandoned terraces, dug at a time when shovels and trucks were less massive.

Pinal, circa 1885

Prospectors who came into the Arizona Territory hoped to find gold; failing that, silver would have to do. Strangely enough, it wasn't prospectors, but four farmers—Isaac Copeland, William Long, Charles Mason, and Ben Reagan—who discovered a fabulous silver lode in 1875. They named their mine Silver King and built their processing plant next to a reliable source, Arnett Creek, four miles from the mine. A settlement called Picket Post soon grew up around the operation. By 1878, its name had been changed to Pinal, after a nearby mountain range, and the thriving community had become an important stage stop.

In 1893, a conservative Congress repealed the Sherman Silver Purchase Act. As a result, the government was no longer obliged to purchase 4.5 million ounces of silver every month at a fixed price, and silver's price sagged. Despite the strong opposition of populists and Western Democrats, the Gold Standard Act was passed in 1900, tying the value of U.S. currency only to gold. This caused a further decline in the price of silver. Although 1896 Democratic presidential candidate William Jennings Bryan was speaking to factory workers and farmers, he could well have been speaking to silver miners when he spoke the famous lines, "You shall not press down on the brow of labour this crown of thorns; you shall not crucify mankind upon a cross of gold." Bryan and the Democrats lost, and the low price of silver sounded the death knell for silver towns such as Congress, Tombstone, and Pinal. The old townsite is barely evident today, and the land has returned to wilderness.

Pinal, 1887

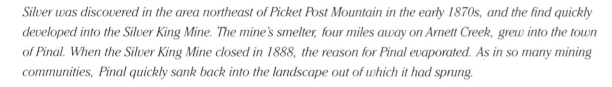

Silver was discovered in the area northeast of Picket Post Mountain in the early 1870s, and the find quickly developed into the Silver King Mine. The mine's smelter, four miles away on Arnett Creek, grew into the town of Pinal. When the Silver King Mine closed in 1888, the reason for Pinal evaporated. As in so many mining communities, Pinal quickly sank back into the landscape out of which it had sprung.

The seeker of ghostly remains can find a faint trace of Pinal between the Boyce Thompson Southwestern Arboretum and Superior, a few miles south of US Highway 60. Unfortunately, there is not a single foundation remaining to confirm the spot where this thriving mining camp once stood. The best way to make sure you are standing at the exact location is to use this photograph to line up Picket Post Mountain with the vertical bank of Arnett Creek in the middle distance.

Kelvin, 1914

The land bordering Mineral Creek, from its confluence with the Gila River at Kelvin and on past Hayden, held greater deposits of copper ore than perhaps any comparable area in the Arizona Territory. Kelvin's neighbors, Ray and Sonora, found themselves perched on top of such an extensive copper deposit that these two small mining towns were quickly swallowed by a gigantic pit (see page 155). The mine at Kelvin never tapped into such an extensive deposit and soon petered out.

Time has all but erased what little existed at Kelvin. A trace of the Gila River can be seen just beyond the pickup. In time of floods, the river inundates the extensive thickets of trees growing in its bed. The majority of people who have chosen to live in the small communities along this part of the Gila are either retired or work in the mine in Ray. One encounters but few Phoenix residents that have bothered to drive State Highway 177 south from Superior through this area so rich in Arizona history.

Clifton, 1905

Early in their history, the mines around Clifton produced as much copper as any in the Arizona Territory. Until Phelps Dodge Corporation built its own railroad to Lordsburg, New Mexico, Clifton merchants had to rely on horse and wagon to bring merchandise into town. Although women at the time wore long skirts, even when they traveled long distances by wagon, it seems doubtful that the woman on this wagon would accompany the driver on such a trip attired in her best hat.

Since Clifton's large mines closed in the mid-1980s, the town seems to have been caught in a time warp of sorts. Its houses are still occupied, although many of the town's stores are shuttered. Most people work, dine, and do their shopping in the prosperous mining town of "new" Morenci, a 10-minute drive away. Notice how the vegetation on the hill has come back since the smelter ceased to operate.

Clifton, circa 1905

On the mountain beyond the plant, notice the five boxcars and, next to the San Francisco riverbed, more cars. Any large-scale mining operation in Arizona, like this one in Clifton, depended heavily on rail transportation. Once a mine showed real promise, railroad companies would consider building a spur to service it; if they did not, the mining company would. Clifton produced such rich ore that Phelps Dodge Corporation was willing to build its own line to connect its operation to the Southern Pacific main line at Lordsburg, New Mexico.

In its move to expand its operation in this vicinity, Phelps Dodge closed the Clifton mines and moved its main operation to Morenci. After the move, Clifton experienced a prolonged decline. Some workers who are employed in the very big dig in Morenci choose to live in Clifton, but the town is still much smaller than it was in its mining heyday. Unlike Bisbee and Jerome, Clifton has not become a tourist attraction. No doubt, this is due to both remoteness and the lack of unusual stories and checkered history that those towns enjoy.

Clifton, 1907

Pinal County was created in 1875. In the early 1880s, the small community of Ray grew up around a mine that had tapped into a rich copper deposit. In those early years, it took awhile to build a proper courthouse like the one seen here. Just who these six gentlemen were has been lost. Notice the leather puttees girdling the legs of the shortest man, yet he is no more dapper than his mates. There was rarely much fastidiousness in Pinal County during these years.

If the automobiles were removed from the streets of old Clifton, the visitor could well believe he or she had returned to a much earlier era. Be not dismayed that the angle of this rephotograph is slightly different from the original. A building now stands at the spot from which the previous photographer took his picture, making it necessary to set up a camera about 10 feet farther south.

Ray, 1913

Pinal County was created in 1875. In the early 1880s, the small community of Ray grew up around a mine that had tapped into a rich copper deposit. In those early years, it took awhile to build a proper courthouse like the one seen here. Just who these six gentlemen were has been lost. Notice the leather puttees girdling the legs of the shortest man, yet he is no more dapper than his mates. There was rarely much fastidiousness in Pinal County during these years.

Ray and its sister community to the south, Sonora, were doomed when, in 1947, Kennecott Copper Corporation began open-pit mining. Within a matter of a few years, the pit had swallowed both towns. Kennecott continues to operate its mine at Ray, where it uses ever-larger equipment. In this photograph, at least seven of the great dump trucks, similar to those used in Morenci (see p. 147), can be seen moving their prodigious loads. Locate these, for the trucks provide a scale by which viewers can better grasp the extent of the operation.

International Standard Book Number: 1-56579-435-4

Text and contemporary photography copyright: Allen A. Dutton, 2002. All rights reserved.

Editors: Jenna Samelson Browning and Martha Ripley Gray
Assistant Editor: Elizabeth Train
Designer: Mark Mulvany
Production Manager: Craig Keyzer

Published by:
Westcliffe Publishers, Inc.
P.O. Box 1261
Englewood, CO 80150
www.westcliffepublishers.com

Printed in China through World Print, Ltd.

No portion of this book, either text or photography, may be reproduced in any form, including electronically, without the express written permission of the publisher.

Library of Congress Cataloging-in-Publication Data:

Dutton, A. A.

   Arizona then & now / text and contemporary photography by Allen Dutton.

      p. cm.

   Rev. ed of: Arizona then and now. Phoenix, Ariz. : Agp Press, c1981.

   ISBN 1-56579-435-4

Arizona — Pictorial works. 2. Arizona — History — Pictorial works.

3. Arizona — History,

   Local. I. Title: Arizona then and now. II. Title.

F812 .D87 2002

979.1 — dc21

                 2002071447

For more information about other fine books and calendars from Westcliffe Publishers, please contact your local bookstore, call us at 1-800-523-3692, write for our free color catalog, or visit us on the Web at **www.westcliffepublishers.com.**

ABOUT THE AUTHOR/PHOTOGRAPHER

Allen A. Dutton, an Arizona native, was born in Kingman in 1922. His grandparents moved to the Arizona Territory in the late 1800s, and the state's history has always fascinated him. Dutton earned a bachelor's degree in art, and, after serving in the U.S. Army from 1942 to 1946, a master's in history with a minor in art from Arizona State University. He went on to study painting and sculpture at the Art Center School in Los Angeles. Dutton then returned to Arizona and found a niche teaching high school history and art. In the early 1960s, he began studying and working with renowned photographer Minor White. Photography became Dutton's primary focus, and he started teaching courses on the subject at Phoenix College, where he later served as head of the department until he retired from academia in 1982.

Dutton's work has been featured in numerous national and international publications, and his collections have been displayed throughout the United States as well as in England, France, Germany, and Japan (where he also taught photography). The Corcoran Museum in Washington, D.C., hosted his most recent show. Dutton and his wife, Mary Ann Enloe Dutton, have three children and currently live in Phoenix.

HISTORIC PHOTO CREDITS

PAGE #	PHOTO CREDIT
Introduction	
3	Don Singer
4	Allen A. Dutton Collection
6	(top) Grand Canyon National Park, Fred Harvey Collection #9654
6	(bottom) Grand Canyon National Park, Detroit Photographic Collection #9841
7	Grand Canyon National Park, Bert S. Mattock Collection #11414
8	Grand Canyon National Park #5305 (Photo by Walter Hamblin)
9	Don Singer
Beginnings	
12	Arizona Historical Foundation
14	Source Unknown
15	Source Unknown
16	Northern Arizona University #NAU 441-4
17	Arizona Historical Foundation
18	Arizona State Archives #97-2647
20	University of Arizona Library Special Collections, Arizona Southwest Photograph Collection, Nogales
22	(top) Source Unknown
22	(bottom) Arizona State Archives #96-4382
23	(top) Arizona Historical Society (Tucson) #14302
23	(bottom) Arizona Historical Society (Tucson) #495
24	Sharlot Hall Museum #CI-TN338P
26	Jerome State Park
27	Source Unknown
28	Source Unknown
29	Arizona State University, Arizona Collection
30	Arizona State University, Arizona Collection

PAGE #	PHOTO CREDIT
Colorado River Settlements	
34	Arizona Historical Society (Yuma)
35	Arizona Historical Society (Yuma)
36	Arizona Historical Society (Yuma)
38	Arizona Historical Society (Yuma)
40	Arizona Historical Society (Yuma)
41	Sharlot Hall Museum #CI-TN194PA
42	Source Unknown
44	Sharlot Hall Museum #RR-136Pb
45	University of Arizona Library Special Collections, Arizona Southwest Photograph Collection, Ajo
46	Arizona State Archives #97-1788
47	Kingman Historical Society
48	Kingman Historical Society
50	University of Arizona Library Special Collections, Arizona Southwest Photograph Collection, Chloride
51	Kingman Historical Society
52	Kingman Historical Society
54	Kingman Historical Society
55	Kingman Historical Society
56	Kingman Historical Society
57	Kingman Historical Society
Mining and Railroads	
60	Arizona State Archives
62	Northern Arizona Pioneer Historical Society
63	Northern Arizona Pioneer Historical Society
64	Northern Arizona Pioneer Historical Society
66	Winslow Historical Society
68	University of Arizona Library Special Collections, The Fred Harvey Collection AZ326, Box 1 Folder 11
70	University of Arizona Library Special Collections, The Fred Harvey Collection AZ326, Box 1 Folder 5
71	Old Trail Museum, Winslow

PAGE #	PHOTO CREDIT
72	Sharlot Hall Museum #CI-TN190P
73	Northern Arizona University
74	Allen A. Dutton Collection
76	Northern Arizona University
77	Phelps Dodge Corporation
78	University of Arizona Library Special Collections, Bridges Collection
80	Sharlot Hall Museum #IN-PR1420P
81	Sharlot Hall Museum #RR 178PF
82	Sharlot Hall Museum
84	Sharlot Hall Museum #ST 106P
85	Source Unknown
86	Sharlot Hall Museum #CI-TN179P
87	Sharlot Hall Museum
88	Sharlot Hall Museum #M300PD
90	Sharlot Hall Museum #CI-TN164PC
91	Sharlot Hall Museum #RR 172PB
92	Sharlot Hall Museum #M-201P
Phoenix	
95	Sharlet Hall Museum
96	Arizona Historical Foundation
98	Arizona Historical Foundation #G-19
100	Arizona Historical Foundation
101	Arizona Historical Foundation
102	Arizona Historical Foundation
104	Arizona Historical Foundation
105	Arizona State Archives #97-0010
106	Sharlot Hall Museum #CI-TN135PD
108	Source Unknown
109	Sharlot Hall Museum #CI-TN145P
110	Joe Wojeck Collection
111	Allen A. Dutton Collection
112	Arizona State University, Arizona Collection
114	Arizona Historical Foundation
116	Allen A. Dutton Collection
117	Arizona Historical Foundation
118	(top) Casa Grande Valley Historical Society, Inc. #71.105.4
118	(bottom) Casa Grande Valley Historical Society, Inc. #91.88.1

PAGE #	PHOTO CREDIT
119	Arizona Historical Foundation
120	Arizona Historical Foundation
121	Sharlot Hall Museum #RR 135P
122	Source Unknown
123	Arizona State Archives #97-5432
124	Arizona State Archives #97-5486
126	Sharlot Hall Museum #MOSG-169PE
127	Arizona Historical Foundation #MC-H282
Ranching and Farming	
129	Sharlet Hall Museum
130	Sharlet Hall Museum
132	Arizona Historical Foundation
133	Pinal County Historical Society
134	Arizona State Archives #95-3528
135	Pinal County Historical Society
136	Arizona State University Special Collections
138	Gila County Historical Museum
139	Graham County Historical Society
140	Arizona Historical Society (Tucson) #2137
141	Eastern Arizona Museum and Historical Society
142	Abrams Collection
143	Arizona State University Special Collections
144	Jerome State Park Collection
145	Jerome State Park Collection
146	Jerome State Park Collection
147	Jerome State Park Collection
148	Arizona State University #RR 333-337
149	Arizona State University #RR 333-337
150	Casa Grande Valley Historical Society, Inc. #79.7.1
152	Graham County Historical Society
153	Graham County Historical Society
154	Jerome State Park Collection
155	Pinal County Historical Society